AF510311

The Necropolitical Production and Management of Forced Migration

The Necropolitical Production and Management of Forced Migration

Ariadna Estévez

LEXINGTON BOOKS
Lanham • Boulder • New York • London

Published by Lexington Books
An imprint of The Rowman & Littlefield Publishing Group, Inc.
4501 Forbes Boulevard, Suite 200, Lanham, Maryland 20706
www.rowman.com

86-90 Paul Street, London EC2A 4NE, United Kingdom

Copyright © 2022 by The Rowman & Littlefield Publishing Group, Inc.

All rights reserved. No part of this book may be reproduced in any form or by any electronic or mechanical means, including information storage and retrieval systems, without written permission from the publisher, except by a reviewer who may quote passages in a review.

British Library Cataloguing in Publication Information Available

Library of Congress Cataloging-in-Publication Data Available

Names: Estévez, Ariadna, author.
Title: The necropolitical production and management of forced migration / Ariadna Estévez.
Description: Lanham, Maryland : Lexington Books, 2022. | Includes bibliographical references and index. | Summary: "Using examples from the United States-Mexico border, Central America, and South America, this book argues that forced migration is not a spontaneous phenomenon, but rather a product of necropolitical strategies"— Provided by publisher.
Identifiers: LCCN 2021044143 (print) | LCCN 2021044144 (ebook) | ISBN 9781793653291 (cloth) | ISBN 9781793653307 (epub)
Subjects: LCSH: Forced migration—Social aspects—America. | Emigration and immigration—Social aspects—America. | Life—Valuation.
Classification: LCC JV6225 .E77 2022 (print) | LCC JV6225 (ebook) | DDC 304.8/7—dc23/eng/20211014
LC record available at https://lccn.loc.gov/2021044143
LC ebook record available at https://lccn.loc.gov/2021044144

A Jorge, in memoriam

Contents

Acknowledgments

I owe my eternal gratitude to the National Autonomous University of Mexico (UNAM), the best place on earth to be a research professor. To the Center of Research on North America's director, Graciela Martínez-Zalce, my gratitude for her support in having this book published.

I am indebted to Vickie Knox, who was generous enough to do a thorough review of the data on the relationship between forced migration and violence, extractivism, and political corruption in Honduras. Her knowledge helped me to improve the discussion significantly. My most profound appreciation to my students at UNAM's Faculty of Social and Political Sciences, Ximena Escalante and Junek Vargas, for helping me gathering data. The Seminar on the Necropolitical Production and Administration of Forced Migration was a laboratory providing me with empirical data to illustrate my ideas. They challenged me honestly and daringly. I'm particularly thankful to Rebeca Vilchis and Rafael Muñiz.

I am profoundly grateful to Jorge Rueda, a loving companion and an exceptional intellectual interlocutor. His praise and challenge to my ideas encouraged me to think more clearly. His encyclopedia-like knowledge also provided me with metaphors that neatly captured the essence of my abstractions. Jorge's love and care were a sanctuary for me while writing this book. The warmth of his home, his legendary breakfasts, and his passion for birds were the perfect peaceful environment for thinking and writing. My heart belongs with him. Always.

My loving gratitude goes to my sister Marión Estévez, who is always there for me.

Introduction

By the end of 2019, around the globe, there were 26 million refugees, 20.4 million convention refugees,[1] 45.7 million internally displaced people, and 4.2 million asylum seekers. The so-called developing countries hosted 85 percent of these 26 million refugees, and 73 percent sought protection in neighboring countries, not in the North. Turkey alone hosted 3.6 million and Colombia 1.8 million. Most refugees (68 percent) came from only five countries: Syria, Venezuela, Afghanistan, South Sudan, and Myanmar (UNCHR 2020).[2]

How did all these refugees come to exist in the first place?

Forced migrants do not just happen to be migrants one day. Before they become migrants, corporations running development projects, extractive industries, and other businesses that harm the environment and destroy communities appear in their homelands. As soon as corporative activities start, contamination, criminal and sexual violence, poverty, deprivation, and lack of resources become widespread. Life eventually becomes impossible because gangs and criminals kill, extort, and rape hundreds in the community, including children; food and air become poisonous or scarce; jobs and opportunities simply disappear. In this context, people have no option; devastation and violence conduce them to situations whereby proper life forms are out of reach, where fleeing is the only chance of survival. However, emigrating becomes *legally* tricky because these people always lacked the opportunities that could grant them papers: education, languages, bank accounts, work experience.

Take the case of Venezuela. Venezuela has an authoritarian political regime facing pressure from Washington for allegedly protecting criminals. At the same time, Venezuela has recently opened up its mining industry to international investment, and the US is not getting any access to it. In 2014, Venezuela approved the Law of Foreign Investment, which allows for international exploitation of gold, coltan, and other minerals in the

Orinoco Mining Arc, which used to be an indigenous and protected land. The Venezuelan government favors Canadian, Chinese, and Russian corporations over American corporations. The Venezuelan government set up in 2016 its own military-run company called Anonymous Military Company of Mining, Oil and Gas Industries to become another investor. Illegal mining is also massive, and Colombian and Venezuelan criminal groups use their terror for these purposes (Ruiz 2018). With this combination of authoritarian and militarized state politics, criminal violence, and resource exploitation, it is hardly surprising that there are 3.6 million Venezuelan forced migrants.

The nightmare continues for people fleeing violence and devastation as the legal means of migrating are impossible to get, so they become commodities in the smuggling and trafficking industries, which moves them along dangerous geographies. Those who survive and reach a country where they can finally apply for asylum have to face Kafkian procedures such as Third Safe Country agreements. An excellent example of this is Turkey. In 2019, Turkey was the country receiving the most significant number of refugees worldwide. In 2016 Turkey signed a Third Safe Agreement with the European Union (EU) to exchange economic privileges. According to the agreement, Turkey has to physically prevent Syrians, Afghans, Eritreans, Iraqis, and Malians from crossing European borders. In 2019, the bulk of world refugees came from Syria (6.6 million) and Afghanistan (2.7), together with Venezuela (3.7), South Sudan (2.2), and Myanmar (1.1) (UNCHR 2020). Turkey receives most deportees from Greece (Ortega-Vázquez 2019).

As we can see from the examples, rich countries rip poor countries of their natural resources, instrumentalizing criminal groups and economies while shutting down their borders to people fleeing this horror. I call this process of making and administrating forced migration the *apparatus of necropolitical production and management of forced migration*. This theoretical framework offers a new approximation to the study of forced migration, seeing it as an element of a broader ontological realm that includes conflict and violence and emphasizing how death becomes lucrative in forced migration processes that involve economic projects within a context of widespread impunity and criminal violence.

The book's theoretical argument is then that necropower enforces the law and a deliberate policy of violence and death to depopulate geographically strategic spaces (such as those rich in natural resources), to produce the forced migrant as a necropolitical subject that is eventually led to dangerous and deadly zones and left to die. The apparatus includes production as well as management strategies and technologies. Legal frameworks work as a hinge that opens the door to exclusion between production and management strategies. This theorization offers a Mexican postcolonial framework for the study of forced migration *vis a vis* an ontological realm plagued with different types of violence—structural, criminal, sexual, and gender-based—aimed at producing profit. Before elaborating the framework in the following chapters, in this Introduction, I shall first locate the book in the broader literature, discussing its particular input: a postcolonial theorization of forced migration in the necropolitical era. I will discuss next the methodological issues and describe the book's structure.

FROM THE BIOPOLITICS OF ASYLUM TO THE NECROPOLITICS OF FORCED MIGRATION: THE STRUCTURAL PLACE OF VIOLENCE AND DEATH IN CONTEMPORARY HUMAN MOBILITY

Critical scholars usually address the coloniality of migration in North America and the Americas from a decolonial point of view (Grosfoguel 2014, Grosfoguel 2017, Herrera Rosales 2018), borrowing from Neo-Marxism and, more specifically, Emmanuel Wallerstein's world system theory. This critical literature focuses on how racism drives the reproduction of American imperialism and coloniality. This book focuses on the making and management of migration worldwide but emphasizing the North American region. However, it departs from the decolonial tradition. It explores what I contend is a Mexican postcolonial view of forced migration, a view situated (Haraway 1988) in a context where migration is systematically produced and managed to reproduce the subordination relations of the postcolonial globalization. It also departs from the Marxist examination of economic structures and actors as neocolonialism, which is at the heart of decolonial research. The book borrows from the Third World Approaches to International Law (TWAIL) (Chimni 2006) to produce critical knowledge about asylum and migration international law. In this context, the book looks at how necropower's legal and policy discourses and apparatuses construct subjectivities perpetuating colonial structures and subjectivities, shaping what Mayblin calls the postcolonial present (Mayblin 2017, 2020a, 2020b, 2020c).

The book then contributes to the refugee and migration literature in three different ways. Firstly, it adds to the research questioning the power issues behind the material, legal, and policymaking of forced migration (Tazzioli 2020, Picozza 2021, Walia 2021). The refugee and migration literature builds on critical border studies and Neo-Marxism to argue that forced migration did not come to exist in a lucky day: colonial structures progressively and systematically produced it "politically" (Picozza 2021), through "border imperialism" (Walia 2021), or over "processes of subjectivation and subjection" (Tazzioli 2020). In the same way, colonial traces in international institutions administrate them through racist laws and policies. In short, "Borders are an ordering regime, both assembling and assembled through racial-capitalist accumulation and colonial relations" (Walia 2021: 2).

Secondly, the book adds to literature analyzing asylum and migration from a postcolonial viewpoint (Squire 2009, Mayblin 2017, Davies and Isakjee 2019, Mayblin 2020a, Mayblin 2020b, Mayblin 2020c, Picozza 2021). This postcolonial literature examines the colonial relationship between countries where conflict and extractivism produce forced migration, and former colonizing powers administrate it from global institutions and national immigration systems. What is specific in this literature is the analysis of migration and asylum discourses, structures, and institutions in a historical perspective to give an account of how the postcolonial present is constructed. Mainstream asylum literature keeps silent about the emergence of non-European refugees and the colonial exclusions and legacies in policy, law, and perceptions of refugees themselves. Refugee studies have not pursued a postcolonial analysis of asylum because it has not incorporated the history of race studies. Notably, it is lacking colonial history allowing for the assignment of different values to different bodies. Theorizing asylum policy in colonial relations implies historical sociology of the development of asylum in the history of colonialism (Mayblin 2020a, 2020b, 2020c).

The book adds to this literature a broader postcolonial context because it does include a historical view of asylum and migration law beyond Europe, specifically how migration governance subsumed the historical asylum regime. It focuses on what I call the *postcolonial space*: space where racial, class, gender, and nationality subordination is widespread, and we find it in the First and Third Worlds alike. Nevertheless, given that violence and profitable death has a key ontological position in this framework, the specific input of this book is the necropolitical conceptualization of the phenomenon of forced migration, which expands the scope of studies merging necropolitical analysis with postcolonial migration (Davies and Isakjee 2019). The importance of this framework is that by placing violence and profitable death at the ontological center with the necropolitics framework, the reductionist view of what constitutes involuntary migration comes to the fore. As I shall demonstrate, more than ever, economic strain, environmental degradation, criminal and sexual violence, and cultural conflict are a result of necropolitical governmentality.

Finally, and more importantly, the specific input of this book is the theorization of forced migration from a Foucaultian and necropolitical methodological and theoretical standpoint. The regulation of migration –a policy intended to define who can enter and remain in each territory is a fundamental subject of biopolitical analysis. Biopolitics has become a recurrent analytical tool for examining migration policy in the context of the securitization of borders post-9/11 (Zylinska 2004, Bastos 2008, Bigo 2002, Bolaños 2009,

Balibar, Mezzadra, and Samaddar 2012, Negri et al. 2017, Campesi 2012). According to Campesi (2012), in general terms, securitization discourse constructs migrants in three different ways. Firstly, migrants are surreptitious transnational actors who pose strategic threats to receiving states, helping to explain why increased border enforcement is necessary. Secondly, migrants threaten the national identity and represent a political threat to the cultural and ethnic social balance, leading to racism and radical identity politics. Finally, migrants are unfair economic competitors in labor markets who profit from the Welfare State's social benefits in Western countries (Campesi 2012). According to Campesi, there are two analytical approaches to migration as a security problem: the biopolitical route around ideas of the state of exception, and the governmentality approach, focused on apparatuses and discourses (Campesi 2012).

In the first case, while Carl Schmitt argued that the state of exception refers to exceptional democratic measures taken in times of political crisis –a "nobody's land" existing between the law and politics. More recently, Giorgio Agamben argued that today the state of exception is no longer an exception, but the way democracies rule. We virtually live in a state of "legal civil war" where life is subordinated to state power and is only present in law through its exclusion (Agamben 2001, 2004). In the second case, governmentality is the rationality of biopolitics. In modern Western societies, this means liberal governmentality, or in its more contemporary form, *neoliberal* governmentality (Foucault 1997: 67). Migration policy—neoliberal governmentality's policy and norms intended to regulate who enters and remains in a given territory—and its underlying racism are fundamental subjects of biopolitical analysis. Scholarly studies of migration and asylum from a biopolitical perspective examine how different apparatuses manage migrants' lives through institutions. Some authors call this the "deportation regime" (De Genova 2010) or the "migration regime" (Mezzadra and Neilson 2013). This regime produces different migration subjects such as the "undocumented migrant," the "asylum seeker," and the "economic migrant."

Biopolitical studies of migration and asylum mainly examine the role of migration detention camps in Australia and Europe, and more recently, the so-called refugee crisis in which thousands of migrants have drowned in the sea trying to reach shore as their boats sank. However, biopolitics scholars reflecting on this death spectacle are beginning to see the deficiency of biopolitical frameworks to look at death as a consequence of "not doing." Vaughan-Williams argued that biopolitics scholars had to look at the negative aspects of biopolitical regulation beyond the law, securing racial purity. The "thanatopolitical borders" is this death-making side of biopolitics (Vaughan-Williams 2015). Consequently, Sara Dehm analyzes international law's role in "state-produced death," particularly regarding how international law distinguishes between citizens and foreigners for allocating rights, leading to a general lack of medical care for migrants, ultimately leading to death (Dehm 2020).

The book does use a Foucaultian methodology borrowing from ideas of governmentality and apparatuses—I shall address methodology in the next section—but departs from the biopolitical framework because profit-making death and violence have an ontological centrality. It borrows from Achille Mbembe's necropolitics. It develops a framework focusing on how neoliberal governmentalities instrumentalize law and policy, or the lack of them, to produce death through cruelty, distress, brutality, and rights exclusion (especially the right to health) that conduce migrants to death or sickness. A growing necropolitical literature examines how law enforcement, or its lack, produces refugees' death in Africa, North America, Central America, and Europe. For instance, in the African context, Ali H. Bhagat defines necropolitics as the States' prerogative to decide who lives and who dies—the state's sovereign right over death in Mbembe's framework, but in the context of *queer* forced migration within the heterosexual and racialized space of Cape Town (Bhagat 2018).

As for North America, Vicki Squire builds on critical borders and migration studies literature to argue that death has become an essential part of contemporary migratory politics on the Mexico-US border. Squire calls "governing migration through death" to the policy relying on physical violence inflicted directly on migrants' bodies (Squire 2017). Andrés Fabián Henao Castro believes the place of necropolitics is the border. At the border, biopolitical technologies meet necropolitics. He looks at the disposable necropolitical apparatuses that make irregular migrants disposable as soon as they cross the border. The border has three characteristics: militarization, social insecurity, and the production of death worlds (Henao Castro 2016). For her part, Mexican scholar Amarela Varela Huerta analyzes the necropolitics of the slaughter of undocumented migrants in Northern Mexico. She claims that migrant massacres are "emblematic" of a "necropolitical governmentality" of migration in Central America. Massacres perform a death spectacle aiming to punish those who disobey the US' territorial and extraterritorial borders (Varela Huerta 2017).

In the European context, John Round and Irina Kuznetsova claim that necropolitics instead of biopolitics is the best way to analyze irregular migration since authorities and society consider them disposable, and nobody cares about their health, job security, or education. The authors believe that it is imperative to theorize the type of death necropower inflicts on migrants. They develop such a framework around the idea of "letting die," revealing that European countries criminalize migrants and see them as carriers of diseases but fail to provide them with medical aid (Round and Kuznetsova 2016).

Similarly, Moniah Bhatia examines how various state actors and agencies act as "street-level bureaucrats" and inflict cruelty and psychological distress on migrants, pushing them into deathly situations (Bhatia 2020). Musarò, for his part, studies how discourses around migration in Europe represent the Mediterranean Sea as a place of permanent emergency or a social, cultural, and political crisis (Musarò 2019). For him, this "military-humanitarian spectacle of the border" obscures the European borders' real politics. Also, examining the Calais Camp, Beth Wallace claims that camps are a neocolonial technology that physically excludes The Other, whom they see as a threat to sovereignty and cultural values (Wallace 2018).

Most of this European necropolitical literature focuses on how death in Europe's maritime borders, particularly the Mediterranean, becomes a media spectacle in which discourses of crisis and invasion obscure the politics of bodies floating in the sea. Scholars argue that these types of politics dismiss Europe Fortress's necropower and sovereign right to make migrants die by enforcing laws and policies legitimizing and prizing cruelty and a lack of empathy for migrants drowning. In their empirical analyses, European scholars focus on what Jenny Stümer (2018) calls "corpse politics," the contested field in which authorities seek, rescue, and bury migrants' bodies abandoned in the sea and make a media spectacle of it (Stümer 2018, Gržinić and Tatlić 2014, Lo Presti 2019). For her part, Marina Gržinić believes migrants can only get a "necropolitical citizenship" because only when they are dead, they become citizens-citizenship allows authorities to bury migrants in European soil and avoid the expensive cost of body repatriation. She claims that racialization serves capital because it is a differentiation process between citizens (by birth and acquisition), noncitizens (refugees, asylum seekers), and documented migrants in Europe. Racialization discriminates all of them differently because labor markets impose a violent selection process among migrants according to race, class, and gender. At the bottom are those who only manage to enter Europe and obtain citizenship when they have died (Gržinić and Tatlić 2014).

This necropolitical literature on forced migration lacks the structural view of the necropolitical approach. It looks at the tanathopolitics of contemporary neoliberal governmentality of forced migration, as Vaughan-Williams pointed out. Reviewing biopolitical literature on borders and migration, Repo (2016) argues that thanatopolitics is "

As I discussed elsewhere (Estévez 2018a), what distinguishes necropolitics from biopolitics is not correctly the "making die" part. Instead, it is the structural and power analysis of the relationship between postcolonial power and subaltern subjects and countries, the capitalistic activities profiting from the death of the poor and the dispossessed, turning them into commodifiable nomad subjects. A structural analysis is what necropolitical studies of asylum and forced migration discussed above lack: an analysis of the uneven power relations forcing some people—the racialized and gendered individuals coming from poor countries—to become migrants, and allowing others—rich countries in Europe, North America, and Oceania—to become the designers of racist laws and policies that administrate death in the borders between the colonial and the colonized countries. Most necropolitical literature has been, in fact, an examination of the thanatopolitics of the biopolitical governmentality of migration.

However, this is changing. Some postcolonial asylum literature uses a necropolitical lens to look at welfare provisions for refugees in different contexts (Davies, Isakjee et al. 2017, Mayblin 2020a, Mayblin, Wake et al. 2020). Mayblin, for instance, analyzes asylum seeker welfare support in the UK, saying that impoverishing and deliberately preventing asylum seekers from accessing the basics of life—clothing, shopping, eating, transport, personal grooming, socializing, desire to work—is a form of "slow violence" that progressively leads to deathly scenarios. They claim that theorizing this type of necropolitics as slow violence allows us to see deprivation of basics not as a new phenomenon or something that violates liberal values, but "as the logical contemporary expression of historically embedded colonial/ modern, racially hierarchical worldviews which have their roots in the colonial enterprise" (Mayblin, Wake et al. 2020: 108). Similarly, analyzing migration camps in Europe, especially the Calais Camp, Thom Davis, et al. make a vital claim regarding the necropolitics of asylum, saying that migration biopolitics, as well as structural violence presented as "violent inactions," are means of migration control, "necropolitical brutality" (Davies, Isakjee, and Dhesi 2017). They call "violent inaction" to the French state's deliberate decision to prevent asylum seekers in the Calais camp from accessing formal services, leading directly to thousands having to live in hazardous spaces. In both cases, the focus is structural because they see the slow speed of "violent inaction" and "slow violence" as a continuum of colonial violence and subjugation of the racialized other. In the North American context, Varela Huerta's edited volume also addresses the structural causes of forced migration, the murder of asylum seekers and refugees involving the legal and the illegal economies, and the instrumentalization of urban infrastructure for killing asylum seekers. However, like the studies mentioned above, it lacks a more systematic approach to what specific technologies necropower uses to produce or manage forced migration (Varela Huerta 2020).

This book aims to fill this gap in the necropolitical literature by adding the postcolonial view on the historical coloniality of asylum law and the structural nature of contemporary violence and death inflected to forced migrants. The book contends that necropower as the power to make die for capital reproduction is inherent to neocolonial powers' neoliberal capitalism.

Therefore, necropower in the apparatus of forced migration refers to a network of private and state actors that include third and first-world countries. First World necropowers use different death technologies in their strategies. While in low-income countries, the government works with organizations such as the drug cartels and various groups of hitmen and assassins for hire, rich countries are in association with corporations that profit from legal death management industries: weapons, mining, prisons, and tourism industry. Therefore, first-world countries' necropower works not above or below the law *but through the law*. Necropower facilitates necrocapitalistic activities according to a necropolitical *metalegal* standard that I call the *pro morituri principle* instead of *pro hominem*. Death is a commodity central to policy and corporative profit. Making migrants die is functional and lucrative for state and market reproduction.

Therefore, the book offers a conceptualization of postcolonial powers as the first-world type of necropower, which I call the rule of law necropower. This approach constitutes a lengthy and systematic necropolitical framework for the study of migrants' commodification due to a process of production, legal categorization, and management of precarious mobility. It seeks to conceptualize forced migration as a process of production of living and disposable commodities—the forced migrants. Consequently, it examines the causes of forced migration and the policy and law intended to manage it. It sees forced migration as an ongoing process produced by the international community and private actors ranging from corporations to organized crime.

The necropolitical apparatus of production and management of forced migration interprets forced migration beyond asylum as a politico-legal category. It is a structural and legal examination of the link between extractivist capitalism and the closing of borders in Europe and North America in a global migration context. The apparatus refers to how first-world necropowers lead people subjected to criminal and legal violence, death, sexual and labor trafficking, slavery, and the criminal economy to deathly situations in their countries of origin or when they try to cross increasingly securitized and dangerous borders. The apparatus's technologies, such as legal systems, guarantee that the poor and marginalized are disposable and die as they try to migrate. Necropower makes undocumented migration illegal, putting obstacles to asylum, and carrying out massive and express deportations.

A FOUCAULTIAN METHODOLOGY FOR A NECROPOLITICAL THEORIZATION OF FORCED MIGRATION

In terms of methodology, the book borrows from TWAIL too. It relies on a poststructuralist methodology to look at forced migration production and management. It operationalizes a Foucaultian methodology for looking at forced migration as an apparatus of necropolitical governmentality with various technologies-necropolitics. The theoretical approach is necropolitics, but I operationalize a methodology based on Michel Foucault's concepts of governmentality and apparatus. These concepts are usually related to the study of biopower.

Biopower is Foucault's late work on power and the subject. He claimed that the right to decide life and death was a privilege of the sovereign, a power derived from *patria potestas*, which was the power that the father in the Roman family had to decide whether his children and slaves should die. The sovereign could decide if his subjects went to war, which meant that he could, indirectly, decide their death. If someone refused to obey, the sovereign could directly decide if the subject died. This sovereign's right was "the power of life and death" (Foucault 2013).

Foucault argued that there was a profound change in the power over life by the seventeenth century, taking two forms: (1) an "anatomo-politics of the human body," which consisted in treating the human body as a machine, that is, focusing on "its disciplining, the optimization of its capabilities, the extortion of its forces, the parallel increase of its usefulness and its docility, its integration into systems of efficient and economic controls" (Foucault 2013: 43); and (2) a "bio-politics of the population," that is, a power "focused on the species body, the body imbued with the mechanics of life and serving as the basis of the biological processes: propagation, births and mortality, the level of health, life expectancy and longevity, with all the conditions that can cause to vary. Their supervision was affected through an entire series of interventions and regulatory controls" (Foucault 2013: 41–42).

Biopower modifies the sovereign's right *to let live* and *to make die*, essentially inverting the relationship: instead of *letting live* and *making die,* the state exercises the right to *make live* and *let die*. It focuses on processes specific to life itself, such as birth, death, reproduction, migration, and disease. At the same time, the technologies used are also different: medicine, statistics, birth control, and policy, anything intended for use as a means of population control (Foucault, Senellart, and Collège de France 2008, Foucault, Senellart, and Davidson 2007, Foucault 2000). As Foucault claimed, it is, in fact, "indirect murder" since without killing intentionally, entire populations die as a consequence of the state not doing anything on their behalf (Foucault 2006a). Power fragments the biological field into a hierarchy of races, leaving those at the bottom to die (Foucault, Senellart, and Collège de France 2008, Foucault, Senellart, and Davidson 2007, Foucault 2000).

The law has an essential role in biopolitics. Ordinarily, the law pertains to the sovereign and disciplinary powers: while the first results in legal codes, the second implements these codes institutionally (Foucault 2006b, Foucault et al. 2007). Nevertheless, there is a strategic use of law in biopolitics; norms become more important than the judicial system itself. It does not mean that law or its institutions tend to disappear but that the law increasingly serves as a norm—intended to impose conformism and homogenize—and that judicial institutions are more integrated into neoliberal governmentality through a continuum of apparatuses with regulatory functions. Biopower uses the law as a technology of domination, that is, to "determine the conduct of individuals and subvert them to certain ends of domination and objectivizing of the subject," and technologies of the self, which "permit individuals to effect by their own means or with the help of others a certain number of operations on their own bodies and souls, thoughts, conduct and way of being, so as to transform themselves in order to attain a certain state of happiness, purity, wisdom, perfection, or immortality" (Foucault 1982: Html page). Therefore, analyzing law as part of neoliberal governmentality and its apparatuses is critical.

Governmentality

Now, the rationality of biopower is governmentality. In modern Western societies, this means liberal governmentality, or in its more contemporary form, neoliberal governmentality (Foucault 1997). For Foucault, government means "to govern things" (Foucault 1997: 218). The techniques of government are not exclusive to the state since they constitute a group of actions that influence the possible actions of other subjects, or the actions exercised to dominate pleasure or desire: "Government of children, government of souls and of conduct, government of a home, of a State, or of oneself" (Foucault 1997: 81). Knowledge and expertise are crucial in the current government's strategies and technologies ruled by neoliberal discourses (Rose in [Rose, O' Malley, and Valverde 2006]). Foucault points out that "governmentality" refers to three things:

1. The ensemble formed by the institutions, procedures, analyses, and reflections, the calculations and tactics, that permit the exercising of this very specific, albeit complex form of power, which has as its target

population, as its principal form of knowledge political economy, and its essential technical means apparatuses of security.

2. The tendency, over a long period and throughout the West, that has steadily led to the pre-eminence of this type of power over all other forms (sovereignty, discipline, and so on)—which may be termed "government"—resulting, on the one hand, in the formation of a series of specific governmental apparatuses and, on the other, the development of a complex of knowledges (*savoirs*).
3. The process or, rather, the result of the process through which the state of justice of the Middle Ages became the administrative state during the fifteenth and sixteenth centuries and gradually became "governmentalized" (Foucault 1997: 219–220).

Clearly, in Foucault's framework, government does not refer to the institution of government but to "an activity that undertakes to conduct individuals throughout their lives by placing them under the authority of a guide responsible for what they do and for what happens to them" (Foucault 1997: 219–220). As we can see from the above definition, in order to differentiate political governmentality from other types of governmentality, Foucault referred to the first as "Governmentalization of the state," which "takes place in the framework of state institutions, treating them not as individuals or a labor force but as a population, a 'general system of living beings' or 'the human race.' The governmentalization of the state is 'the way in which the behavior of a set of individuals became involved, more and more markedly, in the exercise of sovereign power'" (Foucault 1997: 68). This process has turned the justice state—the sovereign state ruled by the law—into the managerial state, which administrates life through specific techniques. It involves using apparatuses deploying strategies and technologies, and producing subjectivities intended to regulate life (Foucault 1997: 70–71). The governmentalization of the state also involves the creation of apparatuses and the use of knowledge intended to regulate life (Foucault 1997: 70–71). One of this expert knowledge in contemporary neoliberal governmentalities, particularly the law. I, therefore, analyze asylum and migration *vis a vis* the neoliberal governmentality, which aims to produce and manage death while profiting from it through the necropolitical apparatus of forced migration.

Apparatus

According to Foucault, an apparatus (*dispositif*) is a network of discursive and non-discursive elements, such as laws, institutions, and infrastructure, with the specific function of maintaining power. In the era of neoliberal governmentality, "apparatuses are as follows: inclusive, as they tend to include more and more elements; permissive since they can be added to; and exclusive, since they eliminate" what they are aimed at (Foucault 2006: 66–67). Agamben (2009) has broadened this concept claiming that: "Further expanding the already large class of Foucaultian apparatuses, I shall call an apparatus literally anything that has in some way the capacity to capture, orient, determine, intercept, model, control, or secure the gestures, behaviors, opinions, or discourses of living beings." He adds that what comes between a living being and an apparatus is a subject: "I call a subject that which results from the relation and, so to speak, from the relentless fight between living beings and apparatuses" (Agamben 2009: 14).

Apparatuses bring together several regulatory technologies, such as governmental offices, councils, courts, law offices, civil society organizations, and the law. Even though the law pertains to the complementary sovereign and disciplinary powers, in neoliberalism, there is also a strategic use of the law in which norms become more important than the judicial system itself (Foucault, Senellart, and Davidson 2007). It does not mean that the law or its institutions tend to disappear but that the law increasingly serves as a norm—intended to impose conformism and homogenize. Judicial institutions are more integrated into neoliberalism, biopolitics' rationality, through a continuum of apparatuses with regulatory functions. Apparatuses play a crucial role in disciplinary power—the power intended to make docile bodies—and in biopolitical governmentality, that is, neoliberalism.

As stated above, apparatuses work through implementing strategies deploying regulatory technologies such as governmental offices, councils, courts, law offices, civil society organizations, and the law. For Foucault, strategies are "the totality of the means put into operation to implement power effectively and to maintain it" (Foucault 1982: Html page). Also, strategies are the specific means employed to "attain a certain end" (Foucault 1997: 346). As for technologies, according to Foucault, a technology is "practical rationality governed by a conscious aim" (O'Farrell 2005: 58). There are four types of technologies: production, sign systems, power, and the self. According to Foucault (1982), "The contact between technologies of domination of others and the self, inform governmentality." Technologies of domination "determine the conduct of individuals and subvert them to certain ends of domination and objectivizing of the subject." Technologies of the self "permit individuals to effect by their own means or with the help of others a certain number of operations on their own bodies and souls, thoughts, conduct and way of being, so as to transform themselves in order to attain a certain state of happiness, purity, wisdom, perfection, or immortality" (Foucault 1982: Html page). The technologies used by biopower are biopolitics.

While looking at how legal categories have changed as a consequence of the colonial relation in the asylum regime, I "problematize" the notions of the refugee and the forced migrant. According to Foucault, "The archaeological dimension (of discourses) made it possible to examine the forms themselves; its genealogical dimension enabled me to analyze their formation out of the practices and the modifications undergone by the latter" (Foucault 1985: 12). Problematization then allows for the examination of how particular issues become the subjects or objects of a particular discourse. In this case, I carry out a problematization of the category of the forced migrant, as a continuation of the colonial notion of the refugee and the asylum seeker.

General Issues

The book deploys a Foucaultian methodology to examine how forced migration is produced and managed in the global necropolitical governmentality through different strategies and technologies, where asylum law is critical. In order to develop this argument, the book first examines the idea of necropower in general, with its first and third world versions and their application to migration studies. Next, it discusses forced migration production, which includes two strategies: *forced depopulation* and *lucrative death*. The book then argues that the international asylum and refugee regime's subsumption to the global governance of migration produces the forced migrant as a refugee replacement. It goes on to argue that legal categories facilitate forced migration management strategies. There are three such strategies: *the transnational necropolitical nomosphere*, the *pro morituri asylum laws*, and the *pockets of disposability*. The data includes twenty qualitative interviews with asylum seekers, lawyers, NGO activists based in El Paso, Texas, and Tijuana, Baja, California, where I carried out fieldwork. I also used legal databases and institutional reports for the statistics and journalistic works to describe specific regional and country contexts.

I use the term forced migrant instead of emigrant and immigrant. The migrant refers to leaving a country and entering another one, reflecting the ambiguity of this process, which is open-ended, circular, and spatially defined. The forced migrant includes asylum seekers awaiting legal decisions; people fleeing criminal-related violence or displaced by economic projects; deported persons expecting the best moment to try to go back to the wealthy nation they were expelled from; and people who are on their way to a rich country.

In addition, throughout the book, I refer to "First World necropower" and "Third World necropower." Using the First World/Third World terminology could seem outdated and probably reaffirming a civilizational binarism. However, it has critical epistemological implications, and it is commonly used in postcolonial approaches to international law, such as this one. Rajagopal argues that using the Third World category as a category referring to power relations rather than a geographical reference could be a counter-hegemonic epistemological practice.

He claims that the Third World has been understood as an ideological category referring to a group of states in bipolar politics; a geopolitical category referring to countries that are different from the First World in terms of the political and economic organization; and a category marking a historical process of countries that lived under colonial rule. More importantly, Third World has been used in popular language to refer to "a certain set of images: of poverty, squalor, corruption, violence, calamities, and disasters, irrational local fundamentalisms, bad smell, garbage, filth, technological 'backwardness' or simply lack of modernity" (Rajagopal 1999: 1–2). For Rajagopal, the former understanding of the Third World is a result of the first three, in which the state as a geographical unit is central.

Rajagopal believes that the Third World category should be used without reference to any specific geographical area but "as a counter-hegemonic discursive tool that allows us to interrogate and contest the various ways in which power is used" (Rajagopal 1999: 19). This is because the Third World category reveals a historical hierarchical order that other concepts such as "South" and "developing countries" fail to portray. As Mayblin rightly states, the Third World does not exist as a region or geographical area. However, it captures images of coloniality—poverty, otherness, exoticism—that are useful "for us, as scholars, to allude to a particular discourse (or sensibility, or imaginary) about the world and the differences between the people and places within it" (Mayblin 2020).

STRUCTURE OF THE BOOK

The book comprises four chapters, a conclusion and epilogue questioning the future of mobility post–COVID□19. Chapter 1 presents the theoretical outline framing the production and management of forced migration. It discusses Mbembe's idea of necropolitics widely and my interpretation of a first-world necropower *vis a vis* forced migration, asylum law, and subjectivity. The book presents the ideas of *lucrative death* and the *rule of law necropower* as the core of the necropolitical production and management of forced migration since they secure profit for the legal and the illegal political economies. It defines the idea of the necropolitical apparatus of forced migration, explaining that it has different strategies and technologies for production and management, which are, in turn, mediated by international and domestic asylum legislations. Chapter 2 argues that forced migration does not appear spontaneously one day. Instead, corporations' extractivist activities and criminal violence produce it. These are the production strategies of *forced depopulation* and *lucrative death.* Both strategies aim to depopulate, deliberately, resource-rich geographies by either killing or displacing people. To achieve their goal, corporations, and criminals—with the state's compliance—terrorize people and destroy communities while devastating the environment. In turn, corporations and the state instrumentalize criminal violence against people who protest destruction.

Chapter 3 discusses how the international asylum and refugee regime produces the subject of the necropolitical apparatus of forced migration as a continuation of colonial relations. It argues that neoliberal governmentality subsumed the regime, merging it with the human rights universal system and fragmenting the legal categories of asylum and refugee status into several types of forced migrants, who are not always deserving of international legal protection. Merging and fragmentation allow for the rule of law necropowers' *pro morituri* lawmaking. Chapter 4 discusses how the necropolitical apparatus manages forced migration after corporations and criminals, with state support, produced it. International legislation fragmenting asylum and the refugee into categories undeserving of international legal protection becomes crucial in migration management. It argues that a transnational necropolitical spatialization of law shuts down safe migration routes and directs forced migrants to riskier and more expensive routes handled by transnational organized crime. The necropolitical spatialization of law is what I call the *transnational necropolitical nomosphere*. It produces a geographical bottleneck plagued with crime and natural hazards that kill migrants, ultimately completing the inconclusive objectives of forced depopulation and lucrative death. Finally, those who managed to survive the journey towards North face *pro morituri asylum law*s that make them redundant and eventually disposable in urban spaces the book calls *pockets of disposability*.

The conclusion is an epilogue of the challenges that the 2020 pandemics of COVID□19 imposes on human mobility. It contends that forced migration will not cease, mainly because the global lockdown increased poverty and inequality in already impoverished countries and places where conflict has not stopped. However, the new pandemics will stigmatize human mobility the same way HIV/Aids stigmatized gay sex and drug use. Class, gender, and the race will determine the target of stigmatization. *Zoomism*, a new form of production already in process, will produce two types of subjects: the middle-class *digital nomad* and the deprived *walking waste*. The latter is the forced migrant, whose body will become a biological and not only a racial threat.

NOTES

1. Convention refugee is the person who gets international protection meeting the requirements of the United Nations' 1951 Convention Relating to the Status of Refugees and its 1967 Protocol. A person gets refugee status under the UNHCR mandate if they demonstrate persecution motivated by their religion, nationality, ethnicity, political opinion or belonging to a specific social group. I shall deal with this in depth in chapter 3.

2. COVID□19 pandemics in 2020 slowed down this process during the lockdown, but it is likely to worsen it in the long term it is becoming an extra factor aggravating inequality and poverty as pushed factors.

List of Abbreviations

AALCO Asian-African Legal Consultative Organization
ACLU American Civil Liberties Union
ACNUR Alto Comisionado de las Naciones Unidas
AIDS Acquired Immune Deficiency Syndrome
AMLO Andrés Manuel López Obrador
BBC British Broadcasting Corporation
CEAV Comisión Ejecutiva de Atención a Víctimas
CISAN-UNAM Centro de Investigaciones sobre América del Norte / Universidad Nacional Autonóma de México
CMDPDH Comisión Mexicana de Defensa y Promoción de los Derechos Humanos
CNDH Comisión Nacional de los Derechos Humanos
COVID-19 Corona Virus Disease 2019
CPI Corte Penal Internacional
DACA Deferred Action for Childhood Arrivals
ECHR European Convention on Human Rights
EOIR Executive Office for Immigration Review
EU European Union
FARC Fuerzas Armadas Revolucionarias de Colombia
HIV Human Immunodeficiency Virus
ICC International Criminal Court
ICE Immigration and Customs Enforcement
ICPPED International Convention for the Protection of All Persons from Enforced Disappearance
IDMC Internal Displacement Monitoring Centre
IDP Internally displaced persons
INA Immigration and Nationality Act

IOM Organización Internacional para las Migraciones
IPG Indirect Private Government
IRCA Immigration Reform and Control
MSF Médicos Sin Fronteras en México
MPP Migrant Protection Protocols
NAFTA North American Free Trade Agreement
OAS Organization of American States
OAU Organization of African Unity
OSAC The Overseas Security Advisory Council
OVV Observatorio Venezolano de la Violencia
PEMEX Petróleos Mexicanos
SARS COV 2 Severe Acute Respiratory Syndrome of Coronavirus 2
SIDS Small Island Developing States
TWAIL Third World Approaches to International Law
UAE United Arab Emirates
UN United Nations
UNCAT United Nations Convention against Torture and Other Cruel, Inhuman or Degrading Treatment or Punishment
UNHCR UN High Commissioner for Refugees
UNODC United Nations Office on Drugs and Crime
US United States
USA United States of America
USCIS United States Citizenship and Immigrant Service

Chapter 1

The Apparatus of Forced Migration Necropolitical Production and Management

At the borders of rich countries, migrants and deprived populations are not merely left to die; they have to face deadly scenarios from which they must escape to survive; necropower pushes migrants and the poor towards harmful sites where life is precarious or even impossible. Criminal violence, impunity, and exception push deprived populations out of their homes in resource-rich geographies, turning them into forced migrants. Fracking, mining, the palm and precious woods industries, drug cartels, feminicides, massacres, and political killings of local authorities and human rights and environmental activists are the forces behind the forced displacement of these deprived populations. Furthermore, migrants waiting to have their asylum procedures resolved, or those who have been deported and are waiting for another chance to cross the border flee to the peripheries and other urban spaces unsuitable for life, places such as garbage dumps and sewage tunnels. As we can see, migration does not start with people's desire to leave, but they slowly destroy corporations settling in a community. The process goes on with a long journey ending at asylum claims that could take years. Forced migration is always an ongoing process, not a fixed phenomenon.

The book advances the hypothesis that forced migration is the process of becoming and being a person in transit and exile as a consequence of being at the center of the *apparatus of forced migration necropolitical production and management*. The apparatus of forced migration includes the set of policies, laws, institutions, and political discourses producing a profit in a legal context in which habitat devastation is legal, but mobility is a crime. It has a production phase and a management phase. On the one hand, in its production phase, the apparatus forces people to flee their homes if they are in the way of development or extractive projects. On the other hand, in its management phase, the apparatus manages internal and international forced displacement through trafficking and smuggling, instrumentalizing the asylum regime and migration laws to dispose of at the margins of wealthy nations. Altogether production, management, and the legal asylum and refugee regime construct a *subjected* subject: the forced migrant. The production of forced migration uses two strategies: *forced depopulation* and *lucrative death*. Management utilizes different strategies altogether: *the transnational necropolitical nomosphere*, the *pro morituri asylum laws*, and the *pockets of disposability*. Legal categories of forced migration, especially asylum and the refugee, are the discursive constructions conducting the forced migrant to deathly spaces.

Chapter 1 discusses the theoretical framework upon which this theoretical work builds. Firstly, it discusses Achille Mbembe's (2011) theory of necropolitics and its origins and situated interpretations, including my concepts of the *necropolitical governmentalization of the state* and the *rule of law necropower*. Consequently, I will first discuss Mbembe's necropolitics and private indirect government (necropolitical governmentality). Next, I shall characterize the necropolitical legal system. I will then discuss the different types of capitalism in the necropolitical era, distinguishing the economic necropractices in the first and third worlds. It goes on to examine necropolitics' subjectivities, emphasizing its disposable collective subject, forced migration. Finally, the chapter explains how this framework makes for the idea of the necropolitical apparatus of forced migration.

THE MANAGEMENT OF DEATH: FROM THE NECROPOLITICAL GOVERNMENTALIZATION OF THE STATE TO THE RULE OF LAW NECROPOWER

Scholars from Africa and Latin American have pointed out that Foucault's understanding of biopolitics does not explain the power over life and overall death in the same way everywhere. They believe that biopolitics is inadequate for assessing the politics of life in the third world, where non-state violence regulates death, not life. In other words, while biopower creates lifestyles determined by class and race (Gržinić and Tatlić 2014), power in the third world—*necropower*—generates a *politics of death*, a form of *necropolitics* (Mbembe 2011, Valencia 2010). In the view of scholars from peripheral countries, while biopolitics is a fundamental starting point for the analysis of relations of domination, in the context of the third world, it proves inadequate because the strategies and technologies used in the relations of domination have very different and radical effects. Biopolitics and necropolitics are not in opposition, however. Instead, necropolitics is a postcolonial view intended to differentiate the effects of power over life in a context of colonial power, which is determined by xenophobia, racism, sexism, and classism. In this context, what is at stake is not lifestyles but the reproduction of the political economy that commodifies death and instrumentalizes massacres, homicide, and feminicide for profit.

The essential necropolitics thinker is Cameroon-born philosopher Achille Mbembe, who coined the term (Mbembe 2003, 2011); he argues that biopolitics is not enough to understand how life becomes subordinated the power of death in Africa. He claims that the proliferation of weapons and the existence of worlds of death—where people are so deprived that they become the living dead-indicate a politics of death (necropolitics) rather than a politics of life (biopolitics) is in operation. Mbembe examines how permanent states of exception and sieges reformulate the sovereign's right to kill. For Mbembe, "the ultimate expression of sovereignty resides, to a large degree, in power and the capacity to declare who may live and who must die. Both killing and allowing to live constitutes the limits of sovereignty, its fundamental attributes. To exercise sovereignty is "to exercise control over mortality and to define life as the deployment and manifestation of power" (Mbembe 2003: 11–12).

Mbembe argues that military operations and the right to kill are no longer exclusive to the governmentalized state and that the regular army is not the only means to exercise the right to kill. In this scenario, the new actors are urban militias, private armies, and private security officers with access to death techniques and practices. The proliferation of necroempowered entities, together with widespread access to sophisticated technologies of destruction and the consequences of neoliberal socioeconomic policies, makes concentration camps, ghettos, and plantations unnecessary disciplinary devices since they can be substituted by massacres, which can take place anywhere and at any time (Mbembe 2011).

As for governmentality, Mbembe refers to this in necropolitical contexts as an Indirect Private Government (IPG). He defines this as: "an unprecedented form of social structuring that currently characterizes African states. This form of government arises in the context of great shortages, deinstitutionalization, generalized violence and deterritorialization. It is the result of a brutal review of the relations between the individual and the community, between the regimes of violence, those of property and the tax order" (Mbembe 2011: 79). IPG is the "exit of the State," that is, the state's abandonment of its duties towards property and economic regulation, allowing the entrance of new private actors such as private armies.

Mbembe's African reading of Foucault has heavily influenced other scholars writing from the periphery's perspective about the role of governmentality in the generation of violence. For example, Valencia (2010), who studies necropolitics in border cities, agrees with Mbembe in his reinterpretation and radicalization of Foucault's biopolitics. Like him, he believes that today death rather than life is at the center of biopolitics, which effectively transforms it into necropolitics. However, she moves beyond Mbembe to say it is not enough to simply introduce an analysis of the deadly impact of neoliberalism and private necroempowered entities' activities. Valencia claims that necropolitics has to be geopolitically and context-specific. Consequently, she offers a reflection on necropolitics in hyperconsumer societies, where extreme violence and hyperconsumerism serve as structuring elements in the construction of dissident—although illegal-subjectivities resisting state power.

She argues that if biopolitics controls life processes, capitalist demands have transformed life and all associated processes-such as death-into commodities. In hyperconsumerist societies, bodies become commodities, and their care, conservation, freedom, and integrity are related products. As a commodity, life is more valuable when subject to threats, kidnappings, and torture. For Valencia, illegal drug corporations wield a parallel power of oppression. They have effectively become a parallel state that reconfigures biopolitics and uses technologies called necropractices—radical actions designed to inflict pain, suffering, and death through murder, torture, and kidnapping—to seize, retain, and profit through exercising the power of making die.

THE NECROPOLITICAL GOVERNMENTALIZATION OF THE STATE

While I agree with Valencia (2010) and Mbembe (2003, 2011) in most interpretations, I believe that necropower is not a parallel state but rather a *necropolitical in places producing forced migration governmentalization of the state.*[1] It entails the state's delegation of domination technologies-the means of coercion-to criminal gangs for population control through murder, torture, persecution, human trafficking, and sex trafficking. The target is not the regulation of reproduction but to enforce political power over subjects in a context where corruption and impunity are so widespread that everyone is vulnerable to violence and death. It uses political discourses such as the war on drugs or the security crisis to regulate death; public spaces' securitization is the central strategy, and the criminal economy is the principal motivation. The actors of the necropolitical governmentalization of the state include cartels but also gangs, politicians, some branches of the army, police officers, the American government funding the drug war, the Canadian government allowing for mineral extraction, and transnational corporations investing in mining and agriculture. The regulation of death is productive, as Valencia (2010) explains, but also in the sense that expertise in death technologies is a valuable commodity for producing situations of terror and chaos that eventually favor corporations' extractivist activities. The necropolitical governmentalization of the state conduces the police and the military to situations where expert management of the technologies of death is advantageous because people receive miserable salaries, and the market and consumption subordinate ethical principles. The irregular use of the law is critical in the necropolitical governmentalization of the state.

To understand how the law works in the necropolitical governmentalization of the state, David Delaney's theory of the *nomosphere* is useful. The nomosphere "refers to the cultural-material environs that are constituted by the reciprocal materialization of 'the legal,' and the legal signification of the 'socio-spatial,' and the practical, performative engagements through which such constitutive moments happen and unfold" (Delaney 2010: 24). For him: "Nomos is not simply law, but is the immediate form in which the political and social order of a people becomes spatially visible. Order is sustained through the concreteness of spatial divisions and orientations. Therefore, law is not contingently oriented by sovereign decision, but essentially legitimated through the concrete orientation of space" (Delaney 2010: 30).

The nomosphere is the material and the spatial world of the law. It refers to how legal discourses and norms give meaning to places and subjects. It is the result of the interaction between different elements: (1) the socio-spatial construction and legal materialization of given ideologies (*nomoscapes*), that is, the legal wrapping of legal systems; (2) the symbolic spaces (*settings*) where legal framing gives functionality and meaning to space; (3) legal situations, which are the practical and temporal engagements of individuals with the social and material world in a particular moment within a legal field of meaning and power; (4) the norms and rules (*traces*) that constitute the signifying elements of legal spaces, such as asylum and migration laws, but also human rights treaties and penal codes; and *legal subjects*, the agents with different power margins that perform the interactions that ultimately construct places such as the citizen, the police officer, and the refugee (Delaney 2010: 30). Providing this definition, forced migration management in the necropolitical nomosphere is different in the first and the third worlds.

In the governmentalization of the state, the nomosphere relies on three legal features: legal formalism as ideology/nomoscape; permanent irregular spaces/settings (physical and symbolic), particularly the collapse of the public/private divide; and the instrumentalization of norms/traces and their legal categories such as asylum seeker, for accumulation of capital. Firstly, a specific feature of legal formalism is norm production, such as adhesion to human rights treaties and new criminal types such as the undocumented migrant and forced disappearance. However, legal formalism does not necessarily lead to enforcement, and impunity has been pervasive. While norm production is rich, judicial authorities fail to investigate disturbances such as human rights, making them invisible—feminicide is an example. Impunity relates to the operational irregularity resulting from the normalization of disturbances, such as the penetration of criminal gangs at all government levels. Apart from these dystopic expressions of law, necropolitical nomospheres also include norms and policies that conduct people to deathly scenarios plagued by irregular nomic figures, like norms facilitating deportation, border shutdown, militarization, mass expulsions, child vulnerability due to family separation, and exposure to illness and violence.

Secondly, legal formalism allows for the establishment of many permanent irregular legal spaces. Delaney (2010) does not conceptualize irregular legal spaces, but I believe that irregularity and illegality characterize some nomospheric spaces in necropolitics. Irregular legal places include the illegal but tolerated and well-known spaces such as safe houses and legal and institutional settings that law enforcement officials working with criminals use as safe houses. Safe houses include state-run migrant detention centers where migration officials or police officers detain men and women in transit and hand them over to criminals for ransom or trafficking purposes. Irregular nomospheric spaces are possible, among other things, due to irregular nomic figures that make disturbances recurrent and even normalized situations, that is, the systematic but not necessarily generalized phenomenon of law enforcement officials working for criminals. Human rights violations occur in the public domain, that is, the political-state arena. Criminal activities are not considered public because legal discourse leads to the belief that they do not occur in the political-state sphere.

Human rights violations in necropolitical nomospheres occur in a nebulous area between private and public settings; the structural impunity affecting the entire legal system obscures these violations' magnitude. Human rights violations' invisibility has two fundamental causes: (a) the spatial collapse of the public/private setting to identify state attribution in responsibility for human rights; and (b) structural impunity, which varies from country to country (see chapter 2 for the Mexican case). According to the public/private division permeating human rights discourse, criminal activities occur in the criminal economy and do not constitute a social problem because they happen in the realm of state policy. In many countries where forced migration takes place, the public/private divide is no longer clear. The blurry nature of this realm serves to obscure the dynamics of power behind human rights violations, as indicated in the Bourbaki Report, which states that in the *narcowar* "human fatalities" are not produced in "the domain of torts" (criminal) and the "domain of legal order" (agents of state power), but in a hybrid form (Equipo Bourbaki 2011: 9).

This intertwining of the state and the criminal is what scholars of mafias have named *intreccio*, which means "more than reciprocity between the mafia and the State; it indicates a vast grey area in which it is impossible to determine where one ends and the other begins" (Schneider and Schneider 2003: 33–34). Nevertheless, the dense intertwining of mafias and the state is not unitary (Schneider and Schneider 2003: 31), and this generally implies a high level of internal inconsistency (Schneider and Schneider 2003: 33–34). Auyero (2007) calls this inconsistency the "grey area of power," which implies a fusion of the violent activities of perpetrators and those who should prevent these (Auyero 2007: 32). For Auyero, this grey area is both an empirical object and an analytical lens that directs attention to a murky area in which normative borders dissolve, enabling state actors and political elites to promote, tolerate or participate in producing violence (Auyero 2007: 32). Human rights violations occur in the grey area and are not registered. The necropolitical nomosphere's grey area of power becomes an obstacle for asylum seekers in countries like the US. The grey area of power obscures the state's unwillingness and incapability to protect their clients in the event of forced depopulation and lucrative death. It also constitutes the spatialization of death in the *transnational necropolitical nomosphere*—see chapter 4.

Finally, legal categories' instrumentalization for necropolitics is related to what Esposito (2005) calls "immunization." He claims that the refugee status, framed in national and international procedures for claiming asylum, becomes an immunization that makes contemporary migrants redundant, residual, and disposable. He draws an analogy between the politics of life and the human body's immune system, saying that the latter fights exogenous threats the same way biopower fights "pathogen" forms of life-threatening the white majority. He then distinguishes between politics over life and politics of life (Esposito 2005). Asylum law and its regime are politics over life, operating as an immune system that defends the body –the population-through negative means that eventually turn against the system itself.

As we know, in medicine, immunization requires the introduction of a nonlethal dose of the pathogen to the body, which creates antibodies and eventually excludes the pathogen. The meaning of this for asylum is that the pathogen—the contemporary forced migrant—is not eradicated from the body (society) by forbidding migration as a whole but by enforcing a law that creates the categories that negate the pathogen, such as legality, asylum norms, temporary protection, and forced migration typologies. Progressive or changing community immunization occurs when policy and legal reforms create or reaffirm categories that negate new forms of migration (Esposito 2005). Therefore, asylum law is a form of immunization against the threat of pathogenic groups (economic migrants and asylum seekers) since it does not negate migration as such; instead, it creates the categories that negate its existence (Esposito 2005).

The Rule of Law Necropower

While the necropolitical govermentalization of the state characterizes third world necropower in Latin America, this does not mean that necropower is exclusive of these countries.[2] European scholars use the concept to analyze the administration of death in the so-called second world (former socialist countries) and the fourth world (the first world's urban spaces where migrants, the poor, and ethnic minorities dwell). In these contexts, necropower instrumentalizes illness, social and environmental abandonment, and legal and symbolic borders (Gržinić and Tatlić 2014, Valverde Gefaell 2016, Giroux 2009, 2014, Nixon 2011, Berlant 2011, Kwate and Threadcraft 2017, Davies 2018).

Gržinić claims that biopolitics is the specific conceptualization of neoliberal governmentality exclusively reserved for the first world since, in the second world (that of the now ex-socialist countries) and the third world (Asia, Africa, and Latin America), capital has transformed the regulation of life into the regulation of death under its extreme social conditions. Necropower regulates life under productive death considerations, reducing people's lives to mere existence (Gržinić and Tatlić 2014). For Gržinić, there are abysmal differences between biopolitics and necropolitics. While the former produces "good lifestyles through the abandonment of regulatory infrastructure—health, education, human capital formation—the latter controls and capitalizes death through the war machine." Since the regulation of life in the First Capitalist World produces "lifestyles," moving from biopolitics to necropolitics implies a qualitative change in the conception of death, which is twofold: actual death by massive impoverishment and symbolic death by the interventions of capitalism in the social, the political and the symbolic. However, in the first world, there are also traces of necropolitics that are invisible and hidden. The dismantling of social policy for citizens and the exploitation, deportation, and marginalization of migrants from the Second and Third Worlds in the Schengen territory are also necropolitics (Gržinić and Tatlić 2014).

Valverde Gefaell (2016) sees necropower more comprehensively; she includes white populations and the marginalized groups of Gržinić's fourth world, although her conceptualization fails to explain the difference between necropower and biopower in the Spanish context. She claims that neoliberalism has dismantled Spain's social state through neoliberal governmentality, the state of exception, and self-government techniques leading automatically to death management. Valverde Gefaell (2016) defines necropolitics as "a policy in which life is the object of calculations, in which the nonprofitable (dependent, sick, chronic, elderly, homeless) are left to die and blamed for their situation, for being a burden on society and not becoming entrepreneurs" (Valverde Gefaell 2016: 23).

Strictly speaking, Valverde Gefaell's interpretation is incorrect because she is defining what Foucault called "thanatopolitics"—already discussed in the introduction. In order to effectively conceptualize first world necropower, Valverde Gafaell would have to emphasize the consortium of state power with private entities producing, or profiting from, death-drug traffickers, militias, supremacist groups, or even corporations in charge of managing and negotiating death technologies such as weapons, penitentiary centers, and gentrifying real estate. Instead, she analyzes the thanatopolitics of the neoliberal governmentality of health (Valverde Gefaell, 2016: 28). However, she does emphasize a feature central to first world necropower: the spatialization of violence and disposability through legal-as opposed to criminal and illegal-actions and policies enshrined in bills, executive orders, proclamations, and legislation. Valverde Gefaell argues that "the city through the laws, the police, and who also own the land, buildings, and businesses do everything possible to make their social and commercial use 'legitimate'" (Valverde Gefaell 2016: 28). Legitimacy indicates profit-making.

For his part, Giroux (2009, 2014) defines the US as some sort of necropower when comparing it to a zombie, a being "who is hyper-dead but still alive as an avatar of death and cruelty." For him, the zombie provides "an apt metaphor for a new kind of authoritarianism in which mindless self-gratification becomes the sanctioned norm, and public issues collapse into the realm of privatized anger and rage. The rule of the market offers the hyper-dead an opportunity to exercise unprecedented power in American society, reconstructing civic and political culture almost entirely in the service of a politics that fuels the friend/enemy divide . . ." (Giroux 2009: 2). Giroux claims that "zombie politicians" create forms of corporate and militarized government that make people disposable, people like poor minorities. The mass media reinforce zombie politics with their pedagogy of cruelty, which makes the poor appear as deserving of their fate, encouraging death, suffering, and exclusion (Giroux 2009).

Other scholars focus on space and Mbembe's sovereignty over death to argue for structural violence producing systematic death situations in first world settings, reaching an epistemological view more related to my understanding of first world necropower. Importantly, Nixon (2011) suggests the concept of "slow violence" to refer to the space-specific violence that economic power inflicts on the poor over time, phenomena such as environmental degradation due to toxic waste or industry activities in general. Slow violence "occurs gradually and out of sight, a violence of delayed destruction that is dispersed across time and space, an attritional violence that is typically not viewed as violence at all. Violence is customarily conceived as an event or action that is immediate in time, explosive and spectacular in space, and as erupting into instant sensational visibility" (Nixon 2011: 2). Postcolonial scholars have borrowed from Nixon's slow violence and Mbembe to examine places in geographies where colonial relations are widespread (Mayblin 2020b, Mayblin 2020d, Davies 2018). Davies examines toxic pollution in former colonial geographies such as Louisiana, located in Cancer Alley, a region in the American South where cancer rates are disproportionately high. Cancer Alley includes the former cotton plantation states where former slaves remained after slavery abolition (Davies 2018).

Berlant (2011) takes up Mbembe's idea of sovereignty to propose that racial minorities in the United States are condemned to a "slow death." Slow death refers to the "physical wearing out of a population in a way that points to its deterioration as a defining condition of its experience and historical existence" (Berlant 2011: 95). She argues that sovereignty as control over death includes necropolitical strategies for the management and erosion of the collective life of ethnic minorities. Berlant uses obesity within the African American community as an example of slow death. By classifying obesity as an epidemic and a "disgraceful disease of sovereignty," the North American necropower stigmatizes the culture, habits, and genetics of minorities. It also transfers to individuals the responsibility for their physical care-eating healthy is a personal option and not a symptom of poverty (Berlant 2020). Finally, Kwate and Threadcraft (2017) return to Mbembe to propose the concept of "dying slow" to describe the diffuse and environmental factors of policing through "stop and search." It begins with simple individual encounters and escalates to encompass all the African American community, producing dysfunctional bodies awaiting death.

I argued elsewhere (Estévez 2018) that what distinguishes necropolitics from biopolitics is not the "making die" part, but the structural and power analysis of the relationship between the colonial power and subaltern subjects and countries, the capitalistic activities profiting from the death of the poor and the disposable people, and the role of law and legality in these interactions. Such analysis is missing in some of these authors' analyses (Gržinić and Tatlić 2014, Valverde Gefaell 2016, Giroux 2009, 2014). Other authors go deeper into structural and colonial legacies of contemporary deathly spaces in first world settings (Nixon 2011, Berlant 2011, Kwate and Threadcraft 2017, Mayblin 2020b, Mayblin 2020d, Davies 2018). However, their emphasis is on the slow pace of death production in the postcolonial space and how the violence producing death becomes imperceptible by producing particular subjectivities. My approach is different in that it aims at analyzing the structural and colonial role of the law and related governmentality in producing death. What is specific about violence and death in the postcolonial space of the first world in the necropolitical era is that they always leave a profit.

I define the first world necropower as the sovereignty to administrate death through adherence to the rule of law, the spaces it creates, and the profitability of the deaths it produces. Lon L. Fuller famously listed the features defining the liberal view of the rule of law: generality, publicity, and a set of relatively constant rules. Friedrich Hayek widened this definition, arguing that "government in all its action is bound by rules fixed and announced beforehand—rules which make it possible to foresee with fair certainty how the authority will use its coercive power in given circumstances" (Tushnet 2016: 5). Other liberals, like Ronald Dworkin, also broadened this liberal view with a civil rights approach (Dworkin 1986) and ideas of accountability, fair and general laws, and open government (Bingham 2011).

Therefore, the rule of law's main characteristic is norm production, such as civil liberties or new criminal types such as the terrorist, and the illegal immigrant, among others. Critical legal scholars claim that the rule of law is nothing but an ideology that judges interpret according to their subjectivity marked by class and race (Tushnet 2016), while feminist legal scholars argue that the rule of law has failed to deliver equality for women (O'Donovan 1989). I agree with these critiques. However, the conceptualization of the rule of law necropower requires a closer look at how the law manages death.

I argue that necropower in wealthy countries is the sovereign power of making die along the lines of class, race, ethnicity, nationality, gender, and class, not within states of exception but under the rule of law. The researcher also follows David Delaney's (2010) theory of the nomosphere to conceptualize Valverde Gafaell's (2016) assertion that necropower's law enforcement has spatial implications. The rule of law necropower's nomosphere, therefore, relies on two legal features. On the one hand, it has a nomoscape (ideology) marked by the centrality of classical legal formalism and the primacy of the *pro morituri* principle as crucial means of interpretations. On the other hand, the use of norms and legal categories (traces) for the subjectivation of disposability. Firstly, legal formalism refers to the ways legal reasoning and resolution of disputes inform a system of legal deduction. It requires finding the core principles in a given area of law and resolving the dispute by deductive reasoning based on the starting principles. In his seminal study of the judge's subjectivity and the spatial maintenance of the status quo, Clark claimed that "legal formalism is simple an ideology blocking our appreciation of the more fundamental mechanisms of social and geographical stratification" (Clark 1985: 42). Law is rhetoric, but not empty rhetoric, he claims.

While liberal legal discourses highlight the importance of individuality and life when interpreting and enforcing the law under the customary principle of pro hominine—interpreting the law in a way that brings more benefit to legal subjects. The rule of law necropower always claims to respect the rule of law but interpret and legislate norms through a principle that seeks to leave people to die. It is a *pro morituri* principle, the legal interpretation condemning subjects to death. Like the alleged greeting of gladiators to the Cesar Morituri te salutant, necropowers' interpretation of the law has the imperative of making die all those who are disposable in the terms described by Giroux (2009). Drawing from Clark (1985), judges and other law interpreters "act to ensure economic efficiency" (Clark 1985, 46). The rule of law necropower legislates and interprets the law through norms and policies that conduct people to deathly scenarios, such as laws facilitating deportation, border closing, and militarization, mass expulsions, child vulnerability due to family separation, exposure to illness and violence, construction of ghettos, and ethnic-directed mass imprisonment.

Finally, there is the instrumentalization of legal categories for profit-making death and disposability through the construction of subjectivities. Necropower produces subjectivity through discourses and technologies, and depending on whether life or death is at stake, power objectifies human beings in different ways, as discussed in the last part of the chapter. Defined this way, the rule of law necropower has two particularities: *capital accumulation through lucrative death*; and the use of apparatuses for the *legal spatialization of lucrative death* and *subject disposability*.

NECROCAPITALISM(S)

Capitalism, or rather, radically corrosive forms of capitalism, are fundamental in necropolitics. Contemporary theorizations of capitalism carry adjectives reflecting the complexity of defining what Karl Marx discussed profoundly but when life and death were neither capital productive nor prone to commodification. The incommensurability of neoliberal capitalism and its *ethos* of death are developed in ideas such as: *zombie capitalism* (Harman 2009), which based on Marx's original concepts focuses on the destructive capacity of capital and its power to put us against us themselves; *gangster capitalism* (Woodiwiss 2005), which describes how organized crime in the United States has been successful thanks to the support of transnational politicians, bureaucrats and executives; *ghost capitalism* (Roy 2014), which examines how the demands of global capital have subjected millions of people in India to brutal forms of environmental predation, exploitation, and racism; *narconomics* (Wainwright 2016), which analyzes the productive, distribution, and sale chains of drug trafficking from an economic perspective, including internet sales, diversification of illicit merchandise, social responsibility and mergers between cartels, and *narco-war capitalism*, which suggests that internal conflicts and militarization focus on critical geographies for energy projects and resource extraction (Paley 2014).

While there are many competing interpretations and even complementary forms of contemporary death-driven capitalism—for instance, the book will go back to Paley in chapter 3 to explain the role of drug cartels in necro-capitalistic practices— not all of them include what is familiar to both first and third world necropowers: the exploitation of the postcolonial space's land and ethnic and racial minorities. However, first-world and third-world countries have different necropolitics of capital accumulation. There are four interpretations of contemporary capitalism that best describe necropolitics. Sayak Valencia's Gore capitalism accurately describes the cultural traits of contemporary and illegal forms of capital reproduction that commodify death and human bodies (Valencia 2010). It describes necrocapitalistic activities plagued by criminal violence profiting from illegal commodities, from drugs to human and organ traffic, along the routes of trafficking, smuggling, and forced migration, from Africa and Asia through South America and Central America towards Mexico and the US. Two, Bobby Banerjee's necropolitical capitalism describes how mining and similar corporations displace people, instrumentalizing local criminal violence and state corruption (Banerjee 2008). This type of capitalism describes the extractivist activities of countries like Canada, the US, and Europe. Thirdly, Jackie Wang's carceral capitalism analyses the structural role of policing, incarceration, and municipal government in capital accumulation and the reproduction of white supremacy in the United States (Wang 2018: 13). However, policing and incarceration-driven profit is a model that the necropolitical apparatus of forced migration uses for migration detention in Mexico and the US. Finally, Tyner's necrocapitalism, which relies on dead labor, that is, the mode of production profiting from racial and ethnic minorities' exposure to death at work (Tyner 2019).

Firstly, Valencia (2010) argues that *gore capitalism* is a framework aiming at providing the concepts for the interpretation of reality whereby violence has a central role as a potent market tool, survival means, and self-affirmation mechanism. She takes the term gore from a cinema genre focusing on extreme and blunt violence so that she could describe the third world's current stage of capitalism, in which blood, corpses, mutilated bodies, and captive lives are tools in capital reproduction. Gore Capitalism builds on transfeminism and the author's experience of living in a border city (Tijuana, Baja California, Mexico). It informs globalization's "B Side," that is, the dark side of the global economy, the contradictory and out-of-control dimension of neoliberalism usually found in border cities.

Valencia points out that this economy simultaneously destroys bodies and produces capital, the reproduction of which relies on the speculation of bodies as merchandise, and violence as an investment, a tool that both empowers and provides instant capital—producing dead or mutilated bodies as the merchandise that sustains and justifies itself in the process of supply and demand. In Gore capitalism, murder becomes a transaction; violence a tool; and torture, empowerment. She claims violence as an interpretative category cutting across different dimensions of knowledge and action, with symbolic and actual consequences. Violence becomes a tool of self-affirmation and a means of survival, a way of life, work, socialization, and culture. In her view, violence is a new epistemology, a set of relations tying our time with discursive and other types of practices that originated in the current stage of capitalism-neoliberalism. Gore capitalism elucidates the cultural and social circumstances that make possible the subjectivities that operate and maintain the death worlds.

Secondly, necropolitical capitalism refers to capitalist practices or forms of accumulation that involve dispossession, death, suicide, slavery, habitat destruction, and the general organization and administration of violence. Even though the state remains critical in ensuring the original accumulation, there is no clear line that divides it from the market in postcoloniality since the armed forces are in charge of guaranteeing capital (Banerjee 2008). For Banerjee, necropolitics is a new form of imperialism. The forceful expulsion of peasants, he claims, is followed by control over the natural resources they once owned. He analyses "the effects of the sword of commerce" of colonial sovereignty in collusion with corporations, which together establish states of exception for the creation of death worlds where profit-driven deaths are possible and lucrative. Banerjee builds on Warren Montag's notion of necro-economics—ensuring by the use of force that people are "exposed to death and compelled to accept the rationing of life by the market" (Montag 2005: 11) but claims that this notion fails to acknowledge accumulation in colonial contexts, like states of exception, and its actors, corporations. Hence Banerjee argues that "the fundamental feature of necrocapitalism is accumulation by dispossession and the creation of death worlds in colonial contexts" (Banerjee 2006). For Banerjee:

> The necrocapitalistic capture of the social implies new modes of governmentality that are informed by the norms of corporate rationality and deployed in managing violence, social conflict, and the multitudes. No conflict is tolerable that challenges the supreme requirements of capitalist rationalization—economic growth, profit maximization, productivity, efficiency, and the like. Inevitably, corporate rationality overrules, co-opts, or marginalizes interests that could threaten corporate advantage (Banerjee 2006: Html page).

Thirdly, Wang (2018) draws from criminology, biopolitics, and law to examine the role of the law and policing in the reproduction of the American status quo, defined by white supremacy and mass incarceration. Wang's carceral capitalism analyses how, after neoliberal adjustment measures, state and municipal governments in the US became dependent on "the use of coercive extractive mechanisms that squeezed the people on the bottom for cash" (Wang 2018: 16). Wang claims that local governmentalities plundered the poorest—blacks, Latinos, the unemployed—with taxes but also with "offender-funded policing and punishment" and the "hyper-exploitation of residents by the police by directly monetizing policing or by using fees and fines" (Wang 2018: 21). The funding of the police comes from people's money, so fees and incarceration reproduce policing, which is a necropolicy that neoliberalism supports because law and order are the only sectors where the state may invest and reproduce itself. Finally, Tyner claims that there is a new political economy based on workers' premature death:

> . . . an emergent necrocapitalism in which the valuation and vulnerability of life itself is centered on two overlapping criteria: productivity and responsibility. Capital values those bodies deemed productive (e.g., in a position to generate wealth) and responsible, with responsibility conceived of as the ability to participate fully as producers and consumers in the capitalist system while, simultaneously, not incurring a net loss to the system. Those individuals who are deemed nonproductive or redundant, based on an economic bio-arithmetic, are disproportionately vulnerable and increasingly disallowed life to the point of premature death. (Tyner 2019: xiii)

Summarizing, while necrocapitalism explains the overall context in which colonial sovereignty creates states of exception for corporations' interests, gore capitalism elucidates the cultural and social circumstances that make possible the subjectivities that operate and maintain death worlds. Carceral capitalism and capitalist exposure to death explain capital accumulation through policy directed to blacks, Latinos, and immigrants. Banerjee's necrocapitalism, Wang's carceral capitalism, Tyner's dead labor, and Valencia's gore capitalism allow us to understand the three main economic forces of capitalism in both first world and third world necropolitics: (1) extractivist activities that kill habitats, and ultimately kill and displace entire communities resisting corporate activities; (2) incarceration of ethnic minorities and migrants for the reproduction of the state and white supremacy; and (3) violent subjectivities that sell their expertise in death technologies for the conformation cartels, gangs, and militias that cause the terror and chaos that allow corporations to kill and displace people.

THE FORCED MIGRANTS AS THE DISPOSABLE SUBJECT OF NECROPOLITICS

So far, the chapter has discussed Foucault's work on biopolitics, governmentality, apparatus, strategy, and technology in order to present Mbembe's postcolonial critique of biopolitics. It argued that there is necropolitical governmentality administrating the death that necro and gore capitalisms produce. Like neoliberal governmentality, necropolitical governmentality uses several apparatuses deploying strategies and technologies for its specific purposes. An essential strategy for the administration of death in necrocapitalist activity is the apparatus of production and management of forced migration.

The apparatus of forced migration has two phases that require different features of the necropolitical governmentality. The first one is the phase of production, which is initialized by necropolitical activities (mining, development projects, drug trafficking and production, trafficking, and smuggling). While accumulating capital, legal and illegal corporations instrumentalize gore activities and subjects (*sicarios, maras*). People who survive this chaos flee for their lives and become forced migrants. Necropowers produce forced migration and administrates it through such strategies as impunity, policy, and legal categories that include some and make most people disposable.

According to Henry A. Giroux, "what has emerged in this new historical conjuncture is an intensification of the practice of disposability in which more and more individuals and groups are now considered excess, consigned to zones of abandonment, surveillance, and incarceration" (Giroux 2014). For him, the "neoliberal politics of disposability" deprive people of social care, basic income, and even recognition, and throw them in zones of abandonment within the US and its political borders. Migrants, minorities, the homeless, the poor young folk, and the unemployed find themselves in zones that are "sites of rapid disinvestment, places marked by endless spectacles of violence and supportive of the neoliberal logics of containment, commodification, surveillance, militarization, cruelty and punishment" (Giroux 2014). Drawing from Giroux, disposability is the construction of specific subjectivities instrumentalized and disposed of with the cruel approval of governments and society alike. Power produces subjectivity through discourses and apparatuses, and depending on whether life or death is at stake, biopower and necropower objectify human beings in different ways. This chapter argues that the necropolitical apparatus of production and administration of forced migration produces the forced migrant as a disposable subject.

BIOPOLITICAL SUBJECTIVITIES

According to Foucault, there are three modalities of objectification of power through which human beings become subjects: the forms of research that we call sciences; the dividing practices by which the subject is separated within his own body or divided from others, and the techniques through which human beings are willing to become themselves subjects. In biopolitics and necropolitics, subjects are usually a mixture of the three. Biopolitics' predominant subjectivity is *homo economicus*, although jurist Giorgio Agamben argued for a legal version of the neoliberal subject, which is a subjected subject: the *homo sacer*. In necropolitics, the *homo economicus* subject is dystopian, the *Endriago subject*, but there is also a subjected subject: the forced migrant.

The Homo Economicus

In the first place, according to Foucault (2004) *homo economicus* is not the subject of plain English liberalism. This *homo economicus* is purely neoliberal because it is rooted in human capital theory, which in turn brought liberal economic analysis to an entirely new field: labor. Neoliberalism's new interest in work incorporated the missing part in their approach to economic production—land, capital, and labor—and made human behavior the object of economic study. However, labor is not an abstract category for neoliberals—as in Marxism—but a rational decision made by individuals who locate scarce resources. Labor is an economic behavior that the person that works practices, implements, and calculates (Foucault 2004). Looked at this way—assuming, as liberals and neoliberals do, that capital is everything that is the source of future income—then salary is the income resulting from investing in human capital, which is made up of all the physical and psychological factors that allow someone to earn their wages. It has biological elements and requires proper investment in education and mobility (that is, the decision to migrate).

For the worker, their labor is their very own capital, a skill inseparable from the person who owns it. The inherent character of human capital makes it only evident that humans are themselves machines that cannot become alienated, which is the basis of the political and class struggle features of Marxism: workers do not own the means of production—the machines—and can never own the product of their work. On the contrary, the human seen as a machine means that they produce a profit, which is the business itself. The human is a social and economic unit functioning as a self-producing business. The *homines economici* of neoliberalism are then entrepreneurs of themselves, and they are their capital, producer, source of profit, and generator of their satisfaction. The new *homo economicus* is both consumer and producer (Foucault 2004).

The Homo Sacer

In the second place, Italian philosopher Giorgio Agamben contributed to Foucault's neoliberal subject, arguing for a neoliberal subject. He reflected on the subject of today's state of exception. Agamben claims that today the state of exception is no longer an exception but the way democracies rule. We now effectively live in a state of "legal civil war" in which life is subordinated to state power and is only present in law through its exclusion. Central to Agamben's State of Exception is the idea of the *homo sacer* (Agamben 2001, 2004). Agamben compares human life in Foucault's biopolitics with the Greek concept of Zoe, the simple life separate from and opposed to political life, or Bios. Agamben identifies the origin of the inclusion of Zoe in political power in the figure of *homo sacer*. The *homo sacer* is a political-legal figure from the Ancient world that refers to a person who has been accused and convicted of a crime, and while they cannot be sacrificed, anyone who kills them will not be accused of homicide. These individuals are left entirely unprotected by the law, and their inclusion is solely a result of their exclusion. The bare life of the homo sacer is subject to the political only by exception (Agamben 1998, 2001, 2004).

For Agamben, the *homo sacer* is the person who can be killed but not sacrificed. It is the first figure to establish the biopolitical power of the sovereign state since it subjectivizes "bare life" not through its inclusion in the legal order but through its exclusion (Agamben 1998). For Agamben, refugees serve as the best representation of the new *homo sacer* since they are only included in the political and legal domains using their exclusion and can be killed without this being considered homicide. The refugee embodies the concept of the "bare life"; purely biological human existence with no political value, and for this reason, the protection of such life is removed from the political sphere and becomes a strictly humanitarian concern. Therefore, detention camps for refugees are the new concentration camps and serve to express the totalitarian sophistication of contemporary biopolitics. Immigrants in general, but asylum seekers in particular, have become the embodiment of the idea of the *homo sacer* since they are people who exist only because they are outside the law due to their being undocumented or unprotected. I contend, however, that the refugee's conditions that Agamben describes do not apply to name contemporary asylum seekers and refugees, whose bodies are commodified and disposed of (alive or dead), that is, whose lives are lucrative. These new conditions are better described in the subjectivities produced in necropolitics.

NECROPOLITICAL SUBJECTIVITIES

The neoliberal *homo economicus* and even the *homo sacer* have their dystopian, shadow, illegal, and even criminal versions determined by conditions of coloniality and, therefore, of necropolitics. In such contexts, not all individuals can compete and reach neoliberal standards of investment in human capital, and many individuals' situation goes beyond exclusion; they are disposable, and their deaths are not sacrificial but lucrative. Mbembe claimed that neoliberal violence was transforming the subject in different ways to those of the first world. In Africa, neoliberal restructuring of the economy comprised the dismantling of the state and its consequent withdrawal from public services and social security. Neoliberal adjustment led to the entrepreneurship of bureaucrats who sold services to the highest bidder, and the spread of mercenaries. The social crisis led in turn to a crisis of the regime of subjectivity or the "shared ensemble of imaginary configurations of 'everyday life' imaginaries which have a material basis that in turn produced more violence" (Mbembe 1995, 324). Necropolitics' main subjectivities are the Endriago and the forced migrant.

FOR THE PEOPLE WHO HAVE BEEN REJECTED AND MADE DISPOSABLE BY NEOLIBERALISM, DO THEY HAVE ANY 'CHOICES' IN NEOLIBERALISM?

The Endriago Subject

An "economic decision" would be becoming a "successful case" in the illegal and criminal neoliberal economy—drugs and the biomarket, which includes drug, human, sex, and organ trafficking. Millions of people—primarily men—"choose" to become entrepreneurs in this economy and invest in necrocapital, such as weaponry and torturing skills. Those who are already out of the legitimate market, such as racial Others excluded because a long history presumes their inability to be rational, inventive, and industrious as the more "civilized" races, are more likely to be drawn to them in this criminal neoliberal economy. These men become hitmen (*sicarios*) or even mafia leaders (*capos*).

They are the necropolitical *homo economicus* that Mexican philosopher Sayak Valencia (2010) called the Endriago subject. Valencia argued that capitalism is a system of production but a cultural construction as well. Its dynamics create cultural patterns and subjectivities that sustain and reproduce the means of production. The cultural patterns of gore capitalism build on the subversion of the meaning of work caused by the post-Fordist organization of labor. Valencia argues that the post-Fordist contempt towards labor, culture, and the working class in general, subverts the traditional processes of capital reproduction, replacing labor as a meaningful social activity with consumption, even in extraordinarily deprived and marginalized places. Social pressure for consumption and widespread frustration among the young who cannot reach the socially demanded consumption levels make the criminal economy and violence a market tool.

Since work is not a socially valued activity anymore, young men who need to feel competent as providers in a hyperconsumption dynamic look for "work" in the gore industry. Gore jobs include killing, drugs, kidnapping, and the sex trade. Gore jobs become an alternative because there is also a subversion of the humanist project that had prevailed in western and westernized societies. Consumerism replaces humanism. Since goods instead of self-realization through work are more socially accepted and valued, the ethical limitations for engaging in gore activities disappear. In hyperconsumerism, ethics becomes redundant. It becomes the loser's protection. In other words, the economic imperative replaces the Kantian categorical imperative (Valencia 2010).

The Endriago, as Valencia calls this subjectivity, is a mythical character in the book *Amadis de Gaul,* which belongs to Spanish medieval literature. Endriago is a monster, a hybrid of man, hydra, and dragon. The Endriago is a tall, strong, and agile beast that inhabits infernal lands and produces great fear in its enemies. Valencia borrows the term "Endriago" to conceptualize the subjectivity of men who use violence as a means for survival, a self-affirmation mechanism, and a work tool. Endriagos kill and torture for money, but also to seek dignity and reaffirmation as men through a "kamikaze logics." Valencia claims that given the social and cultural conditions prevailing in Mexico, it should not surprise that Endriagos use gore practices to fulfill consumerist demands since they are subverting the feeling of failure evinced by material frustration. The Endriago is the dissident subjectivity resisting power. However, resistance does not mean legitimate resistance: Endriagos continue to be neoliberal *homo economicus* who take entrepreneurship to its last consequences, resisting the neoliberal state, but in a dystopian way (Valencia 2010).

The Endriago subject is usually a male who has been left out of the neoliberal "global village"—the unemployed, the drug addict, the migrant, and the unskilled worker who has been unable to access the legal means to achieve neoliberal success. In other words, the prototype of this subject is the "loser" of the neoliberal system. The loser of the system is the corporality of a complex of neoliberal violence informed by subjective, power, structural, and cultural issues. The Endriago subject as the necropolitical *homo economicus* explains how and why many racialized and dehumanized men are willing to become *sicarios* and capos, and why as part of their human capital, they use rape and feminicide against women. This necropolitical subjectivity makes lucrative death possible, as we shall see in chapter 2.

The Forced Migrant

Another economic decision could be emigrating, probably without documents. Through what Mbembe calls the management of the multitudes, thousands become disposable. Management of the multitudes is a type of governmentality consisting of "The extraction and looting of natural resources by war machines," which "goes hand in hand with brutal attempts to immobilize and spatially fix whole categories of people or, paradoxically, to unleash them, to force them to scatter over broad areas no longer contained by the boundaries of a territorial state. As a political category, populations are then disaggregated into rebels, child soldiers, victims or refugees, or civilians incapacitated by mutilation or simply massacre on the model of ancient sacrifices. At the same time, the 'survivors,' after a horrific exodus, are confined in camps and zones of exception" (Mbembe 2003: 34).

While the Endriagos' economic choices have to do with self-affirmation in a patriarchal system where consumerism equals success, not all subjects can be dystopian entrepreneurs of themselves. In the context of the management of the multitudes, what moves subjects is "forceful hope." The necropolitical forced migration production and management apparatus employs a series of legal categories that simultaneously include some forced migrants and exclude most of them, labels such as asylum seekers, convention refugees, persons in need of protection. At the subjective level, these labels are never clear for subjects. In a concise but powerful paper, anthropologist Alice Elliot (2016) questions the legitimacy of distinguishing between these different types of forced migrants, and between forced migrants and the notion of economic migrant. She makes the point that young white Europeans travel without anyone assuming they are economic migrants. However, the forced migration apparatus constantly questions the travel reasons of racialized subjects from Africa, Asia, and Latin America. She claims that while such forces as "hope," "war," or "travel desire" are not the same, they create "paradoxical hierarchies and artificial distinctions" because these forces usually overlap in migration narratives (Elliot 2016).

She argues for a different focus, one that does not look at desperation but at hope in the future, based on these narratives that tell stories of war, violence but also hope, a desperate "forceful hope." Elliot's "forceful hope" wraps up nicely the interaction between personal and structural causes of forced migration. However, its importance goes beyond explaining migration's "pull and push factors." Forceful hope is the subjective basis for life in disposability.

Given the importance of emotions in the biopolitical regulation of life and death, forceful hope helps to explain the motifs of the forced migrant as the disposable subject of the apparatus of necropolitical production and management of forced migration. According to Anderson (2012), in biopolitics, emotions are an "object-target" for manipulating subjects-for example, maintaining optimism amid economic crises. Borrowing from Hardt and Negri's idea of subsumption of life to capitalist production, he claims that "as production extends to all of life, all life must be secured to ensure 'good' circulations amid threats that are imminent to life" (Hardt and Negri 2000: 34). Emotions are part of a manageable life, ontological events leading to new life forms, biopolitics from below. Through apparatuses, biopower intervenes affective capacities and relations, but emotions condition the emergence and development of apparatuses themselves. By managing emotions, neoliberalism conduces peoples' conduct toward certain ends that are productive of capital (Pincheira 2012, Anderson 2012).

Necropolitics is no different from biopolitics regarding the productive role of emotions. Nevertheless, they neither manipulate the same emotions nor have similar outcomes. Biopower regulates such emotions as happiness (Pincheira 2012) and state-phobia (Anderson 2012) to make people responsible for their well-being instead of blaming economic inequality and consumption for their precariousness. Instead, necropolitics is likely to manipulate emotions related to death, like suffering and forceful hope, to understand that these emotions move them either to political idleness or to a migration project, respectively (Estévez 2017). As explained above, forceful hope is a type of painful and desperate optimism produced amid despair, suffering, and disappointment. Forceful hope makes viable illegal means of traveling vis a vis the coercive shut down of legal means of migration, such as asylum. Forceful hope is what moves migrants on their journey.

Forced migrants are the ultimate necropolitical subject because their death becomes lucrative at different stages of their journey and are disposed of when necropowers finish cannibalizing them. However, they resist. Unlike the *homo sacer*, there is nothing sacred about them, or unlike the Endriago, they are not subjects of violence but subjects subjected to the market of violence. Their death is lucrative: along their journey, forced migrants are either commodified to exhaustion or ultimately conducted to deathly spaces and conditions that are profitable too. When people's death is no longer lucrative—say, a deportee from Congo who is ill with Aids and COVID□19 lives in the riverbank of a border city such as Tijuana—further cannibalizing their bodies for profit is not possible. This condition goes beyond the *homo sacer* because exclusion is not legal, is ontological: their bodies have no commercial value anymore. However, at the same time, they continue to live.

That is why they are disposable, or as Treviño (2020) claims disposable commodities. For Treviño (2020), it is clear that migrants' bodies and lives are lucrative, becoming disposable commodities. Treviño claims that migrants in transit are not illegally detained, held incommunicado, treated in a cruel and degrading manner, extorted and sexually assaulted by multiple agents of the Mexican state because they were viewed as a severe risk to the nation's security, or because they endangered the stability of the country. They all suffered various forms of abuse because they were seen simply as a *commodity* with the potential to generate money or a sensation of power, even if it is a momentary sensation; moreover, they were seen as a *disposable* commodity (Treviño Rangel 2020: 108).

Consequently, the forced migrant is the disposable subject of the necropolitical apparatus of forced migration: bodies subjected to death, the criminal market where migrants' life, organs, genitals, and labor force are commodified and exploited to exhaustion. Those surviving death and managing to claim asylum are ultimately clogged in the borderlines between rich and poor countries because they still have hope, as we shall see in chapter 4.

CONCLUSION

The necropolitical apparatus of forced migration is the enforcement of necropolicies for the organization of space for forced displacement and death along the lines of race, gender, and class. It includes two strategies of production: lucrative death and forced depopulation, which produce asylum seekers, refugees, and so-called undocumented migrants. It also includes three management strategies: the transnational necropolitical nomosphere, *pro morituri* asylum laws, and pockets of disposability.

The necropolitical apparatus of forced migration uses strategies and technologies to secure that poor, marginalized, and disposable people die before, during, or while trying to leave their countries. Forced migrants' journey is plagued with criminal enclaves, political killings, persecution, and acute sexual violence and trafficking. They become subjects subjected to different forms of lucrative death that treat them as the disposable subject of necropolitics. Criminal markets devour their bodies to exhaustion, leaving just the cut-offs clogged in the borderlines of rich countries processing their entry as asylum seekers.

NOTES

1. I discuss the necropolitical governmentalization at length in my previous book, Necropolitical Wars and the Biopolitics of Asylum in North America, published in Spanish as Guerras Necropolíticas y Biopolítica de Asilo en América del Norte (CISAN-UNAM, 2018). I assess this concept vis a vis competing ideas such as the state criminal reconfiguration, which is widely used in the Latin American academic and policy literature on organized crime.

2. A more comprehensive discussion of the rule of law necropower vis a vis the necropolitical governmentalization of the state appears in chapter 2: "The Management of Death in North America: From the Necropolitical Governmentalization of the State to the Rule of Law Necropower," in my latest book *Necropower in North America: The Legal Spatialization Of Disposability And Lucrative Death* (Palgrave Macmillan, 2021).

Chapter 2

Producing Forced Migration

Mexican asylum seekers to the United States, the caravans of migrants from Honduras, the exodus of Venezuelans to Colombia, and the thousands of Africans who cross the Mediterranean to Europe are not the subjective expression of spontaneous events. Global displacement is not an individual choice of people aiming to take advantage of rich countries' miserable social programs. Individual migration projects do not start the day a woman with her teenage son or daughter closes the door behind her to go to the US in the hope of saving her teenage son from forcibly joining a *mara* or her teenage daughter from being kidnapped by sex traffickers. Mass migration is the residual outcome of two strategies that necropower's specific forms of capitalist practices and spatializations utilize to de-inhabit geographies rich in renewable and nonrenewable natural resources in the postcolonial space of the third world. Along this process, necropowers profit from deathly technologies such as criminal violence, sex trafficking gang activities, which target men's and women's lucrative death differently. I call these strategies *forced depopulation* and *lucrative death*, respectively. Altogether, these overlapping strategies *produce* forced migration.

The chapter examines the two strategies of production of forced migration: (1) forced depopulation through extractivist activities focusing on mining, fracking, and forest exploitation; and (2) the criminal violence profiting from lucrative death, directly commodifying and profiting from human bodies endangerment or killing. The chapter will discuss each of them with Venezuela and Honduras' examples of forced depopulation and Mexico for lucrative death.

FORCED DEPOPULATION IN THE AMERICAS

The concurrence of forced displacement, economic development, and criminal, misogynistic, and political violence in the same space is not coincidental, although scholars and policymakers study these phenomena separately and without an emphasis on their spatial coexistence (UNCHR 2015, Mestries 2014). This phenomenon is the violent core of what Bobby Banerjee calls necrocapitalism, the profit-driven deaths discussed in chapter 1. According to Mbembe, this type of economy is characteristic of colonial power relations. He argues that "In the regions of the world situated on the margins of major contemporary technological transformations, the material deconstruction of existing territorial frameworks goes hand in hand with the establishment of an economy of coercion whose objective is to destroy 'superfluous' populations and to exploit raw materials" (Mbembe 2000: 284). Mbembe claims that for this type of economy to be buoyant, the "emasculation" of the State and the appearance of different forms of armed groups targeting civilians are necessary (Mbembe 2000).

It is a necropolitics of obtaining "conflict-free" exploitation of natural resources that are increasingly valuable in the modern global economy—minerals used in new technologies and renewable or clean energy sources. Capital accumulation through lucrative death and violence supporting extractivist activities that primordially kill and ultimately displace entire communities is what I call *forced depopulation*. A region of the world that exemplifies the overlapping of capital accumulation through lucrative death, violence, and forced displacement constituting forced depopulation is the Americas. According to the UNHCR, the region of the Americas "became the largest recipient of asylum applications worldwide in 2019" (UNCHR 2020: 38). Citizens from Venezuela and Central America alone lodged 1.6 million between 2016 and 2019 (UNCHR 2020: 39).

Indeed, criminal and gender-based violence are widespread in the Americas: 17.2 killings for every 100,000 population in 2017—the highest since 1990. The region held 37% of the world's total homicides while representing 13% of the global population. While most victims were boys and men (81%), most perpetrators were also males (90%); 1.6 women for every 100,000 population are killed by their partners in the Americas—compared to 3.1 in Africa and 0.9 in Asia. Caracas, Tegucigalpa, San Pedro Sula, and San Salvador are the most violent cities in the region (UNODC 2019). Other types of violence affect the region, such as gender and sexual violence ending in feminicide (Estévez 2016), and typical political murders and forced disappearances in the context of social movements opposing extractivist projects (Vice News 2015).

Although homicide reports consider natural disasters and development projects as displacing forces, the bulk of displacement is related to drug cartels and gangs. As far as monitoring agencies are concerned, gangs and only gangs are to blame for this humanitarian crisis and regional tragedy. However, there is an important fact overlooked in these reports: this region is also very rich in biodiversity, minerals, and other valuable natural resources, and they are first-world-based transnational corporations making a profit out of them.

Journalists have documented well the necropolitics of forced depopulation. British journalist Andy Robinson (2020) claims that new *coup d' états* and political crises in Latin America are related to exploiting a dozen raw materials, including oil, coltan, gas, lithium, and avocados. Traveling around Chile, Bolivia, Colombia, Brazil, and Mexico, Robinson witnessed how displacement and conflict came after the protests against environmental degradation or the killing of activists opposing that degradation or the projects themselves (Robinson 2020). For her part, in her book *Drug War Capitalism*, journalist Dawn Paley (2014) argues that internal conflict and militarization occur in key geographical spaces for energy and extraction projects. Her fieldwork in Colombia, Guatemala, and Honduras indicates these phenomena also coincide with sociopolitical opposition to corporative activities in such industries as oil, gas, and mineral extraction and exploration, large-scale agriculture, hydroelectric projects, and logging (Paley 2014). Colombian scholar Ivan Roa claims that the palm industry in Ecuador and Colombia has facilitated the illegal economy and criminal violence because the necropolitical apparatus of forced migration forces people to sell their lands. If they refuse, the governmentalized State and corporations have criminals to kill them (Castillo 2018).

Paley (2014) argues that the connection between drug wars, paramilitary violence, and gas extraction is no longer rare because corporations use criminals to intimidate opponents and control geographies rich in natural resources. The *combo* of violence/resource exploitation first immobilizes people because they have to face police and military checkpoints and attacks on public transport, shootouts in roadways, and disappearing while traveling. However, as securitization becomes widespread, people tend to flee (Paley 2014: 18). Two countries in the Americas are good examples of forced depopulation: Venezuela and Honduras.

Venezuela

In 2020 the UNHCR reported 4.5 displaced Venezuelans worldwide—93,300 refugees, 794,500 asylum seekers, and 3.6 million Venezuelans living abroad. Most displaced Venezuelans went to Colombia, Peru, Chile, and Ecuador. The UNHCR failed to outline the causes of Venezuelan mass international migration beyond extreme poverty, lack of health services, and food supplies. Scholarly literature claims that since 2015 the State has been incapable of providing essential services such as gas and electricity; by 2018, over 90% of the Venezuelan population lived in poverty conditions. Venezuelans were fleeing because of a "generalized institutional and economic crisis" caused by the plunder of Venezuela's oil-based economy (Valero Martínez 2018,

Gandini, Lozano Ascencio, and Prieto 2019). Understandably, scholars avoid addressing criminal violence because Venezuela does not produce official figures (OSAC 2019). According to the academic-run *Observatorio Venezolano de la Violencia* (OVV, Venezuelan Observatory of Violence), the government lacks a proper crime control and prevention policy.

However, available data—United Nations' figures on crime, OVV's reports, the American government's travel advisory reports—indicates that Venezuela's exodus results from forced depopulation. Venezuelans flee their country due to capital accumulation activities through lucrative death in a political economy controlled by many state-sponsored criminal groups. Criminal violence is rampant in the country's main cities, such as Caracas, the country's capital, giving the State the justification for militarization and further spreading repression. In most parts of the country, criminal groups sponsored by the State speculate with food, services, and valuable commodities such as car parts, cellphones, and medicines (OSAC 2019). Thousands of Venezuelans in this condition have fled to neighboring Colombia, where most Venezuelans have fled—over 1.8 million (UNCHR 2020). In Colombian border cities such as Cúcuta, Venezuelans usually need to sleep rough and work in the informal market. For women, it is worse because smugglers take away their documents and force them into prostitution. While they are missing, they could be in the hands of sex traffickers and eventually killed. About 2% of Venezuelan women are survivors of sexual violence (Battistessa 2019).

In other parts of the country, massive migration occurs amid state-supported criminal control of gold mining, forcing people to cross the border with Brazil. Gold is crucial in finance and the electronics and jewelry industries. The most important gold mines are in South America, particularly Colombia, Peru, and Venezuela. Gold corporations, refineries, and buyers are, on the contrary, in the first world: "Illegally mined gold is 'laundered' and exported, with the help of the corrupt United Arab Emirates, which supply some of the biggest central banks, jewelry companies, and electronics producers in the world" (Verité 2016: 3). Until 2008 the American Gold Reserve and the Canadian Crystallex had a vast monopoly of gold mining in the country. However, the government seized their actives, leaving criminal groups supported by the government to take over in the Amazonas and Bolivar states, indigenous and ecological reservations. Since the US has imposed sanctions on Venezuela's gold, the state-run Minerven C.A. buys gold to criminal groups and sells it to Venezuela's Central Bank, and buyers from Dubai and Turkey rechannel gold sales to avoid American sanctions (Bargent and Rainsford 2020).

About 90% of the gold mining in Venezuela is in criminal hands, but that does not mean that corporations are out of business. Instead, they get cheaper deals to ensure that many armed groups or the State will control social unrest. In Venezuela, armed groups include local *pranatos* (a copy of criminal organization within prisons), the former Colombian guerrillas and criminal groups, Mexican, Italian, Russian, and Chine mafias. For instance, while the US imposed sanctions on Venezuela's gold, the Seattle-based Gold Reserve is getting access to Las Brisas-Las Cristinas, the largest gold deposit in Venezuela, through the Empresa Mixta Ecosocialista Siembra Minera, in which the Venezuelan government owns 55% of the shares. Based in Barbados and a foreign subsidiary of Gold Reserve, GR Mining holds the remaining 45% of the shares (López 2017, Bargent and Rainsford 2020).

In the Orinoco Arch, criminals copied the criminal business model of gold mining used in Peru and Colombia a decade ago. Criminal groups controlled gold extraction, charging small miners a quota or even part of their gold. Refusal to pay could end in death (Verité 2016). An investigative journalistic report argues that "this form of mining links mercury and blood, as well as high levels of deforestation, to human trafficking and the devastation of river basins with forced labor. Profits from this are generally higher than other sectors of illicit economies, such as drug trafficking (that is why some of these agents have migrated to the illegal mining business)" (Teran Mantovani 2019: par. 16). Las Brisas-Las Cristinas is in Bolivar state, the heart of the Orinoco Arch. Bolivar ranked second highest in violence rates in 2019—after Miranda. In 2017, Bolivar ranked fourth, and in 2018, third (Observatorio Venezolano de Violencia 2019). Bolivar state has a border with the Brazilian State of Roraima, where there are thirteen refugee camps for Venezuelans. Thousands of these refugees belong to the Warao indigenous group, disposed of their land ever since the government allowed gold mining in the Orinoco. Those who refuse to leave are threatened and eventually killed. Following the comprehensive definition of refugee of the Cartagena Declaration, Brazil has granted refugee status to 224,000 out of the 900,000 Venezuelans who crossed the border (Boadle 2020). Indigenous Venezuelans in Roraima, however, are having a hard time settling down. Over 100,000 Venezuelans live in Roraima under precarious conditions with no access to health care and other services (MSF 2019). In the State's capital, Boa Vista, and the border city of Pacaraima, they live in park lots and the streets, facing xenophobia (Ramón 2018).

Honduras

Between 2004–2008, violence in Honduras displaced at least one member of each household: a total of 247,000 people; 77% (191,000 people) reported state violence and human rights violations, and 47% accused gangs (IDMC 2020a). According to the UNHCR, violence explains the 275% increase of Hondurans' asylum claims between 2015 and 2018—from 6,844 to 18,860 (ACNUR 2016). Also, 55% of those consulted fled due to death threats, 40%

for the murder of relatives, 13% for extortion, and 3% for the recruitment of children and adolescents in organized crime gangs (Forbes Staff 2019). In 2015 alone, 14,300 Honduras claimed asylum in the United States; however, according to the Yearbook of Immigration Statistics, that same year, they only accepted 1,098 affirmative asylum cases and 309 definitive asylum cases; Honduras ranked eighth in the list of asylum claims' country of origin—41,500 new applications. In the same period, the United States received more than half of Hondurans' asylum claims (24,400), Mexico 13,600, and Spain 2,500 (BBC Latin America and the Caribbean 2020).

Most reports and news argue that conflict and criminal violence are responsible for the bulk of Honduran international displaced persons. Widespread violence as the primary cause of displacement is a recurrent argument in public opinion. Another report points out that while there were only 29,000 displaced persons in 2014, by 2015, the figure increased by almost 600%: 174,000. According to the same report, it was paradoxical that when displacement increased in 2014, homicide rates decreased, showing that criminal violence could hardly be the main displacing force (IDMC 2016). The report's explanation for this paradox is vague, saying that the increase might have to do with worsening economic conditions. In a small piece on extractivist industries in Mexico and Honduras, I argued that given this paradox, the displacement pattern in Honduras suggested that criminal violence was not such a determining factor in forced displacement in Central America (Estévez 2016). A couple of years later, shortly after the Honduran caravans of over 3,500 people, British human rights scholar Vickie Knox came across the article and emailed saying that, based on her extensive empirical research in Honduras, she found that corruption and impunity were contributing to displacement and that this included terrible practices related to megaprojects.

Furthermore, she found that state corruption and corporative activities were some of the various factors, including criminal violence, hate crimes, political repression, and the impact of climate change and extreme weather events that caused forced migration in Honduras. Honduras is rich in natural resources, with 41.5% of its territory covered with forests. However, it is also the third poorest country in the Americas and the second poorest in Central America. The poorest people live in rural areas, which are also the forested areas, where longstanding agricultural, logging, and livestock activities, together with megaprojects, have intensified, leading to widespread deforestation, environmental degradation, water deterioration, and soil erosion. This environmental deterioration has negative consequences on local economies and makes communities prone to natural disasters (Global Witness 2009), so farmers and indigenous groups are organizing against corporative interests in forested areas. Widespread criminal violence occurs in large cities, that is, Tegucigalpa and San Pedro Sula. Nevertheless, it also occurs in rural areas with illegal mining and logging activities, such as the Río Plátano biosphere and La Ceiba district (Lagos Nivárrez 2015). Río Plátano is one of the three major protected areas in the country (Global Witness 2009), and La Ceiba district is near the Pico Bonito conservation area.

There are up to 1500 underway and ongoing megaprojects that include hydroelectric dams, solar parks, mines, agribusiness, and tourism infrastructure. The privatization of natural resources and an aggressive campaign targeting investors since 2009 triggered the multiplication of projects (CESPAD 2018, Lakhani 2020). Corporations own concessions for resource exploitation in over a third of the country's territory. She claims that "the transfer of lands and land concentration in fewer hands leaves people who rely on subsistence farming with no usable land or generating conflict. Displacement is being caused by megaprojects and violence associated with them, but there are major gaps in data and documentation on this" (Knox, forthcoming).

Corruption plays a significant role in this, especially since the *coup d'etat* in 2009. The military and the economic oligarchy overthrew president Manuel Zelaya when he called for a referendum intended to assess a constitutional assembly's viability. Since then, the oligarchy has encouraged policy aiming at international investment in mining and other extractivist industries, with the compulsory inclusion of national corporations. Corruption has facilitated legislation and policy that favor corporations and guarantees secrecy (Chayes 2017, GAIPE 2017). For Knox, this translates to displacement that "can result from forced evictions or from threats and violence against those who resist megaprojects. This violence has various perpetrators, often including the security forces, private security, militias, and criminal groups. The failure to conduct environmental impact assessments and consult local communities can also lead to displacement as a result of environmental degradation" (Knox, forthcoming).

Criminal violence occurs around megaprojects and state economic interests as well, that is, drug trafficking. Since 2009, the national elite, supported by transnational corporations, have imposed several leaders, including current president Juan Orlando Hernández, whose brother, deputy Tony Hernández, was arrested in Miami in 2018 on drug trafficking charges. Honduras is likely to be a narco-state facilitating a land route for cocaine trafficking to the US (Insight Crime 2018). Based on Knox's findings, I contend that forced depopulation in Honduras occurs when "The interests of big businesses and the economic and political elites are protected by corrupt officials and politicians and enforced by state agents, hired killers known as *sicarios* and even private militias" (Knox, forthcoming).

Corruption favoring extractivist projects occurs at all state levels and areas, from money laundering to bribes in Congress, and has international links. Indeed, corruption has become the "operating system" in Honduras with "sophisticated networks that link together public and private sectors and out-and-out criminals—including killers—and whose main objective is maximizing returns for network members" (Chayes, 2018: 3–4). This results in situations where the "government may be paid for land, from which people are then evicted without compensation. Resistance and protest are met with state-sanctioned repression, criminalization and violence, with state security forces and the judiciary used to ensure compliance with megaproject plans" (Knox, forthcoming).

The use of violence and criminalization against those who oppose such projects explains why assassins have killed hundreds of environmental activists since 2010. By 2014, there were massive demonstrations against corporative activities in Río Blanco, the same river that *talked* to environmentalist Bertha Cáceres, who was killed in 2016 (Global Witness 2015, Lakhani 2020). Lakhani (2020: 148) argues that the force behind Cáceres' assassination was what she calls "political femicide," the result of "machismo"—Latin America's institutional and cultural misogynistic culture. Bertha Cáceres was not just another activist but a woman daring to lead a movement defending the rivers; therefore, it was political femicide. Following Lakhani, Honduran necropower killed her because corporations and politicians would not put up with a woman interfering in their businesses.

The violence and criminalization also cause some people to flee, although others stay to fight (Contra Corriente 2019). Internal and international displacement, therefore, comes as a result of forced depopulation's violent forces. To sum up briefly, to dispose of populations that are in the way of resource-rich geographies, forced depopulation as a necropolitical strategy in the production of forced migration relies heavily on violence. Entire communities are either killed or forced to flee because of gangs, cartel wars, and sex trafficking. Although disposing of people either by murder or terror is key, violence has economic aims because necropolitical governmentalities are still neoliberal and seek to make money out of death. The strategy of *lucrative death* is what makes death lucrative.

LUCRATIVE DEATH OF MEN AND WOMEN

Lucrative death is the result of killings perpetrated by, and for the reproduction of, extractivism and illegal markets; and executed by necroempowered subjects that are both the objects and subjects of neoliberalism.[1] Being the direct perpetrator or the victim of lucrative death depends on a person's subjective position in capitalism if we follow James Tyner's (2019) idea of necrocapitalism. He claims that a person's position in capitalism conditions their exposure to death: "Inequalities that are manifest in along the familiar axes of exploitation and oppression (ethnicity, gender, sexuality, and citizenship) materialize inequalities to the exposure and occurrence of death" (Tyner 2019: x). He claims that profits are "increasingly realized through the material death of laborers" (Tyner 2019: xi) who are exposed to chemicals, dangerous working conditions and accidents caused by shortages in safety measures. While Tyner is concerned with "dead labor" in terms of workers' inequalities exposing them to premature death, the term helps us to understand what lucrative death is. Because of their precariousness, the poor, women, and ethnic minorities are more likely to inhabit lands where lucrative extractivism occurs. While corporations make money with resource exploitation, people are killed or displaced. Also, migrants, ethnic minorities, and women are more exposed to trafficking, smuggling, and criminal and sexual violence. Their place in necrocapitalism exposes them to deathly places in situations that are simultaneously profitable for legal and illegal businesses. Extractivism and illegal markets, on the one hand, and necroempowered subjects, on the other hand, are the structural and subjective factors producing death for profit and capital accumulation. Gender, class, race, and sexual orientation inequalities expose people to extractivism, sexual and labor trafficking, and the criminal terror of the illegal economy. Lucrative death is then the productive killing both in terms of capital and the constitutive nature of necrocapitalistic practices.

Mexico

Forced depopulation also occurs in Mexico, making lucrative death even more profitable; in turn, lucrative death makes forced depopulation very profitable because human lives are commodities. In 2006 then-president Felipe Calderón declared war on drug trafficking. By 2012, when President Enrique Peña Nieto took office, militarization was already widespread: and so was death. Shootouts, beheadings, abductions, and massacres involving government authorities and rival gangs were rife, while kidnappings, extortion, forced disappearances, torture, persecution, femicide, rape, and massacres involving civilians became daily occurrences. When Peña Nieto left office in 2018, the death toll (2006–2018) was 250,000, with almost 40,000 people reported missing (Suárez 2019). Since leftist President Andrés Manuel López Obrador (AMLO) took power in December 2018, during 2019, violence in Mexico continued unabated: 34,582 deaths (Rivera 2020). 2019 ended up being Mexico's most violent and bloody year since the drug war started (Rivera 2020). The last three presidential administrations have claimed that criminal gangs were solely responsible for these brutalities and invested significant resources in security and judicial and constitutional reform, among other changes designed to tackle impunity and corruption.

However, none of these measures prevented forced migration from 2016. During this period, Mexicans seeking asylum summed up 111,176 (Estévez 2018). In 2015 alone, 51% of new asylum applications in the United States came from Mexico. It is equivalent to 19,300 people (ACNUR 2017), of which only 657 had an affirmative asylum and 204 a permanent asylum, and by 2016 there were 27,900 new asylum applications (US Department of Homeland Security 2017). According to the Internal Displacement Monitoring Centre (2020), by the end of 2019, 345,000 people were displaced due to conflict and criminal violence. In 2019 alone there were 7,100 (IDMC 2020b). Most displaced people lived in Chihuahua, Nuevo León, Tamaulipas, Sinaloa, Durango, Michoacán, Guerrero, Guanajuato Baja California, Veracruz, and Coahuila states (CNDH 2016). Coincidently, all these are geographies rich in minerals, oil, and new renewable energy sources such as oil and shale gas. Chihuahua, Tamaulipas, and Coahuila. Chihuahua hosts the border city of Juarez, the home of the Juarez Cartel, and the most violent city in the world between 2009 and 2010 (Ortega 2010). *Los Zetas* cartel and the Gulf Cartel controlled Nuevo León, Coahuila, and Tamaulipas (BBC Latin America and the Caribbean 2014). The Zetas are responsible for thousands of the over 61,000 forced disappearances in the country (Souza 2020), and the Gulf Cartel had its leaders protected by local politicians (Rodríguez Cortés 2016) are Veracruz alone ranks fourth in the list of world shale gas reserves and has the country's worst record in violence against journalists (Redacción AN 2016).

Most of these states are on the US-Mexico border, along the Mexican side of a significant shale gas source in Texas known as Eagle Ford Shale Basin (*Cuenca de Burgos,* on the Mexican side). A critical problem with shale gas exploitation is the environmental costs because the process entails a technique known as fracking, which uses between 7.6 and 15 million liters of water and very contaminating chemicals (Bessi and Navarro F. 2015). According to scholar Guadalupe Correa-Cabrera, gas exploitation in Mexico intensified shortly after NAFTA's enforcement, which allowed the state-run oil company PEMEX to grant partial participation of American corporations such as Delta and Halliburton. Infrastructure for shale gas exploitation expanded in Chihuahua but not to the extent it did in Texas or even the border state of Tamaulipas (Correa-Cabrera 2018: 335). Nevertheless, the exploitation of shale gas in the Eagle Ford Shale Basin requires water for 27,000 wells. Water is already a scarce resource in the area, and its use for fracking affects water sources and other productive activities such as agriculture. Water scarcity is leading to increasing protests (Grillo 2014). Correa-Cabrera pointed out that the Mexican government has made significant oil and shale gas discoveries in Tamaulipas state, "further enhancing the region's importance and placing it as a strategic area for hydrocarbons worldwide" (Correa Cabrera 2018: 335).

Correa-Cabrera claims there is a spatial coincidence between economic inequality and global fluxes—the *maquila* industry, extraction and sale of hydrocarbons, migration, and transnational organized crime—in the poorest and most violent municipalities of Chihuahua, Nuevo León, Tamaulipas, and Coahuila states: Matamoros, Reynosa, Nuevo Laredo, Ojinaga, and Ciudad Juárez (Correa-Cabrera 2015). She claims that elites have provoked violence deliberately to force corporations to hire private security in the case of Northern Mexico. Organized crime violence triggering state law enforcement has ultimately displaced thousands who fled to Texas (San Antonio, Austin, Houston, McAllen, Mission, and Dallas) (Correa Cabrera 2018: 337). Most victims of forced displacement in Mexico are precisely people resisting poverty, violence, and environmental devastation—farmers, communities with self-consumption economies, environmental and human rights activists, small business owners, local politicians and government officials, and journalists (CNDH 2016).

A significant number of forced disappearances and murders in these areas involve the Army and criminal gangs. Feminicide has also flourished in these states, with the infamous case of Ciudad Juarez in Chihuahua confirming it (Monárrez Fragoso 2009, Padgett 2014). Women are in the front line of environmental activism, like Josefina Reyes Salazar, an activist for the environment and women's rights in Valle de Juárez. Hooded assassins killed her with relatives because of their opposition to their town's militarization, located in a gas shale-rich area that Texans wanted for a nuclear dump back in the 1990s (Tokar and Oliver 1998). Correa-Cabrera has also demonstrated the link between killings, forced disappearances, feminicide, and displacement, with shale gas extraction in Juárez (Correa-Cabrera 2015, Mayorga 2014).

While forced depopulation explains the cases of Venezuela, Honduras, and Northeast Mexico, lucrative death explains Mexican mafias' success beyond the country's rich geography. In Mexico, the governmentalized state profits from corporative activity as well as human lives. In Honduras and Venezuela, the State is a facilitator of businesses and another competitor, instrumentalizing criminal groups for this purpose. In Mexico, mafias compete against each other for the governmentalized State's preference in an illegal drug political economy, where criminals can use this infrastructure to trade commodified human lives—human trafficking and smuggling, sex, and organ trade, among others. This is capital accumulation through lucrative death.

Capital accumulation through lucrative death simultaneously explains criminal and sexual violence as part of a continuum of colonial, gendered, and racialized violence for securing criminal markets and the commodification of women's bodies while producing forced migration in the context of forced migration depopulation. Using Mexico as its focal instantiation, I suggest that capital accumulation through lucrative dead in the postcolonial space of the third world takes place in two contexts. Firstly, the confrontation between criminal gangs to gain the State's protection for illegal business (drugs and other illegal commodities). Secondly, the systematic violence against women for gaining and dispossessing of their bodies for commodification, on the other. These necropolitical contexts are possible because of the necropolitical nomosphere (explained in chapter 1), a dysfunctional, permanently corrupt, racist, and deliberately deadly legal-spatial site. This third-world postcolonial space secures the impunity of these groups' power technologies: massacre, feminicide, and forced disappearance. Necropolitics gives subjects the control of drug markets and sex trafficking and slavery while subordinating women to the reproduction of the economy as a whole.

In order to develop these ideas, I use several concepts of the necropolitical framework discussed in chapter 1, such as *necropower*, *governmentalization of the State*, *Endriago subject*, and *necropolitical nomosphere*, among others (Mbembe 2011, Estévez 2018, Valencia 2010).

Lucrative Death for the Necropolitical Governmentalization of the State

As stated in chapter 1, I share with Valencia (2010) the idea that "necropower" is a criminal appropriation of the fundamental elements of biopolitics—territory, security, and the population—but disagree with the idea that organized crime becomes a parallel state. Empirical studies provide evidence that the co-opted reconfiguration of the State (Flores Pérez 2012, 2013) causes that at certain levels of government, necropower and the State are a single entity. Criminals serve as the armed wing of state power to regulate death following the reproduction of criminal capital. Although a relationship has always existed between criminals and the Mexican State, as Flores Pérez (2012, 2013) indicates, the war against drugs intensified these links. The drug war placed the armed forces and different police bodies in choosing between money and their lives (*plata o plomo*), leading to a war between cartels to win the State's favor. In chapter 1, I called this the necropolitical governmentalization of the State, and it is the form of necropower in the postcolonial space of the third world.

The necropolitical governmentalization of the State is a racialized process, like the war on drugs in the 1970s. John Ehrlichman, President Richard Nixon's Assistant for Domestic Affairs, confessed to journalist Dan Baum, from Harper's Magazine, in 1994:

> "You want to know what this was really all about?" he asked with the bluntness of a man who, after public disgrace and a stretch in federal prison, had little left to protect. "The Nixon campaign in 1968, and the Nixon White House after that, had two enemies: the antiwar left and black people. You understand what I'm saying? We knew we couldn't make it illegal to be either against the war or black, but by getting the public to associate the hippies with marijuana and blacks with heroin, and then criminalizing both heavily, we could disrupt those communities. We could arrest their leaders, raid their homes, break up their meetings, and vilify them night after night on the evening news. Did we know we were lying about the drugs? Of course we did" (Baum 2016: par. 2).

In the late 1970s and throughout the 1980s, the war on drugs expanded its scope internationally, particularly across Latin America, which remained under the US sphere of influence. In Latin America, the war on drugs continued to be racialized. Using the war on drugs as an excuse, the US militarized security services in Colombia, Nicaragua, and others while allowing an umbrella under which governments criminalized the Marxist opposition for drug production. In Mexico's war on drugs, the situation was no different: it has colonial objectives and a color line. Socioeconomic inequality caused by neoliberal economics and the criminalization of the productive drug chains has led impoverished men to the illegal neoliberal economy in which jobs range from the drug, sex, and human trafficking to torturing, killing, raping, and disposing of bodies.

While in the US, the subjects of antidrug policy and securitization were disenfranchised black men, in Colombia they were impoverished male farmers, often from the indigenous and Afro-Colombian communities. In Mexico, the criminal subjects were frequently dark-skinned, uneducated, indigenous, unemployed urban males—often sexist and violent—who have found the illicit economy sector the dole area for a potentially profitable trade. These males are self-employed as hitmen and drug dealers who conflict with each other and rape and murder women, and trade with their bodies. The authorities believe that in this version of the war on drugs—in which there is also a gender and a class line—different forms of neoliberal subjectivity are at stake, specifically the *homo economicus* and its dystopian version, the *Endriago subject*, which incarnates *sicarios* and gang members, as discussed in depth in chapter 1.

To summarize, what we know as the drug war is a confrontation for the necropolitical governmentalization of the State, that is, a dispute between cartels to receive preferential treatment by the State and its association with the State. However, this dispute has mutated. While at first it was a battle for territorial power and control of the drug market, the economic objectives moved into markets and merchandise with an equal commercial value as drugs, but without the increasing costs in terms of risk and security. This merchandise turned out to be the bodies of women. The commodification of women's bodies, the exacerbation of misogyny, systematic impunity, and the growing risks associated with the drugs trade have transformed women into adversaries in another struggle. This confrontation is parallel to the narcowar and involves the same men fighting for the governmentalization of the State and others who have been or could be the object of narco-violence. It is a conflict in which the victim of the war on drugs is also potentially the victimizer since what is in play is not territory or power or control over the illicit drugs market, but the dispossession of women's bodies for their domination and lucrative death through sexual exploitation.

Lucrative Death through the Dispossession of Women's Bodies

I contend that women's lives are lucrative as much as drug trafficking and extractivist industries. While the necropolitical governmentalization of the State may represent a confrontation in which the subjects competing for "necropower" are criminals battling for preferential treatment by the State, violence against women constitutes a dispute for the control of illicit merchandise. In this case, the enemy and the merchandises are the same thing, women and their sexually commodified and objectified bodies. The control of women's bodies is disputed employing extreme physical and sexual violence since this is the only way women can be dispossessed of their bodies for their commodification in the sex market. Women's bodies are a live product that must be dispossessed through torture and death.

To analyze the role of women's bodies as merchandise, I introduce the idea of dispossession developed by Judith Butler (Butler and Athanasiou 2013). Butler states that there are two types of dispossession: (1) the dispossessed subject in a sense it is decentered from itself, which allows it to form relational connections with others and society; and (2) the deprivation of means of subsistence or "accumulation by dispossession" which radicalizes the "original" accumulation of Karl Marx, referring to "the depredation, fraud and violence," entailed by this activity that extracts natural resources to privatize them and profit from them (Harvey 2004).

For Butler, dispossession in the first sense determines the second, for even when we enjoy rights, we are dependent on a type of governance and a legal system that grants us these rights and limits our actions in such a way that even before the possibility of being dispossessed we are outside of ourselves. We are interdependent subjects whose pleasure and suffering depend from the start on a sustainable environment, and for this reason, when someone is born in conditions of extreme poverty, their life is already dispossessed. In other words, "we can only be dispossessed because we are already dispossessed"

(Butler and Athanasiou 2013: 5). This basic idea of subjective and objective dispossession helps us understand how a misogynistic social environment with structural impunity for sexual and domestic violence creates the possibility for violent and misogynistic subjects to dispossess women of their bodies, so they become slaves, forced through physical violence, deceit and depredation to become sexual merchandise.

The dispossession of women's bodies is directly related to the violent and self-affirmative violent activities of subjects central to the *narcowar*: they use the same techniques of extraction, that is, murder and forced disappearance. However, the dispossession of women's bodies is not between criminal groups disputing control of the drugs market and association with the State, but between violent and disenfranchised men and women who resist being dispossessed of their bodies. The front line in the war for women's bodies is where we find the poorest and most marginalized women of rural and urban areas of the big cities.

These bodies are taken from their owners through physical and sexual brutality, so they are enslaved and stripped of their will using threats against them or their children. After this dispossession, their bodies are used in slavery for sexual commerce or control for domestic or sexual subordination. The war for the dispossession of women's bodies is a war whose existence is reflected in the data but has been invisibilized through structural and selective impunity that shows contempt for women and minimizes their suffering to the point of complete inexistence.

THE POSTCOLONIAL SPACE OF LUCRATIVE DEATH

Lucrative death is possible because there is a necropolitical nomosphere operating throughout the postcolonial space of the third world to maintain: (1) structural impunity and conditions in which human rights violations are invisibilized, especially in the case of women; and (2) the use of forced disappearances, massacres, and feminicide is necropolitics for capital accumulation.

Structural Impunity as Part of the Necropolitical Nomosphere

In countries like Mexico, impunity is not the simple result of incompetence or the inability to investigate. Impunity results from the co-opted reconfiguration of the State, which occurs as a consequence of its criminal "capture." State capture is a form of institutional corruption in which business figures and state agents establish alliances for their benefit, ignoring competition rules and with the explicit objective of establishing economic rules that benefit them personally and are not in the public interest (Flores Pérez 2013). In this way, corruption moves beyond bribes and becomes institutionalized. The co-opted reconfiguration of the State occurs when criminals rather than business figures are responsible for bribing authorities and when criminals control the justice and law enforcement institutions instead of economic institutions and rules. The criminal control of law enforcement institutions means the co-optation of those institutions "responsible for enforcing the most essential normative provisions of the State" (Flores Pérez 2013: 50).

Impunity resulting from the co-opted reconfiguration of the State is an essential feature of the necropolitical governmentalization of the State. According to Mexican authorities (cited in Sullivan 2012), more than half the country's municipalities (60–65%) have been affected by organized crime. Drug cartels have infiltrated and used more than 1,500 cities as their operational bases for kidnappings, extortion, and vehicle theft. For this reason, criminal gangs operate in 980 "impunity zones" without restriction. There are "enclaves" in these impunity zones—which are also those of forced depopulation—where criminal gangs exercise greater territorial control than the State. These enclaves are in municipalities of the regions known as *Tierra Caliente* (Hot Lands—Michoacán, Guerrero, Colima, and the Estado de México), *Triángulo Dorado* (Golden Triangle—Chihuahua, Durango, and Sinaloa), the Isthmus of Tehuantepec (Oaxaca), the Juárez Valley (Chihuahua), Tamaulipas, and the Mexico City metropolitan area (Sullivan 2012: 17, 20). According to the Global Impunity Index México 2016, analyzing data from 2010 to 2012, only 4.46% of crimes ended in a conviction, representing an impunity index of 95%. The "unrecorded" crime rate would drive this figure up to 99% (Le Clercq Ortega and Sánchez Lara 2016).

Impunity is also fundamental to ensure the dispossession of bodies. The global index dismisses impunity in gender-based crimes. However, such crimes as domestic violence, forced disappearances of women, and feminicide occur in states with medium impunity (56–60%), such as Mexico City, Chihuahua, Sonora, and Chiapas; high impunity (65–70%), such as Jalisco, Puebla, Sinaloa, Tlaxcala; and very high impunity (70–76%), such as the Estado de México, Nuevo León, Oaxaca, Tamaulipas, Coahuila and Guerrero (Le Clercq Ortega y Sánchez Lara 2016). These are also zones of forced depopulation.

Domestic violence is also the most frequent crime in Chihuahua and San Luis Potosí, where the level of impunity is medium, which means that authorities investigate less than half of cases. This crime is also among the five most common in Baja California Sur, Nuevo León, Puebla, and Quintana Roo. Even though Chihuahua is a state with medium impunity, it has the highest displacement rates, sexual and domestic violence, and feminicide. Baja California Sur, Nuevo León, and Quintana Roo have very high levels of impunity. Meanwhile, in Nuevo León, the domestic and sexual violence, forced disappearance, and feminicide rates are among the highest in Mexico. The number of preliminary investigations for sexual crimes is highest in Nuevo León, Puebla, and Baja California (2010–2015) (Le Clercq Ortega and Sánchez Lara 2016, CEAV 2016). The impunity index in Puebla is high, and it appears on the list of states with the most significant number of feminicides. Also appearing on the list of states with the highest recurrence of the crime of failure to comply with family support is Chiapas, with high levels of feminicide, and Sonora, with a high rate of forced disappearances.

While the impunity index does not break down information on gender, the crimes of bodily injury and homicide may include sexual and domestic violence and forced disappearance, feminicide, and forced displacement. This allows us to cross-reference information concerning impunity with human rights violations involving women. On the one hand, the crime of bodily injury is among the five most common offenses throughout Mexico, including the ten states with the highest rate of feminicide, the eight states with the greatest concentration of the forced disappearance of women, the nine states with the highest rate of domestic violence and the ten states with the highest number of mass forced displacements: Aguascalientes, Baja California, Baja California Sur, Chiapas, Chihuahua, Coahuila, Mexico City, Guerrero, Guanajuato, Hidalgo, Jalisco, Estado de México, Michoacán, Morelos, Nayarit, Nuevo León, Oaxaca, Puebla, Querétaro, Quintana Roo, San Luis Potosí, Sinaloa, Sonora, Tabasco, Tamaulipas, Tlaxcala, Veracruz, Yucatán, and Zacatecas. On the other hand, the crime of homicide is among the five most recurrent in Chiapas, Guerrero, and Sinaloa, where impunity ranges from medium to very high and where feminicide is most prevalent (Le Clercq Ortega y Sánchez Lara 2016).

Forced Disappearance, Massacre, and Feminicide as Technologies of Death

Lucrative death's battlefield, to put it in such terms, is semilegal and characterized by the collapse of the public-private divide in the exercise of violence and the attribution of agents responsible for human rights violations, as stated in chapter 1. In such a scenario, we cannot expect the discussion to be battlefields or front lines. Instead, three technologies of lucrative death characterize the dispossession of women's bodies: forced disappearances, massacres, feminicide.

Forced Disappearance

In the war for the necropolitical governmentalization of the State, the victims are military personnel and police as well as indigenous peoples, racial others, activists, migrants, and young people who engage in no political activity. The International Convention for the Protection of All Persons from Enforced Disappearance (ICPPED and the Inter-American Convention on the Forced Disappearance of Persons) sanctioned persons' forced disappearance. The former establishes that: "'enforced disappearance' is considered to be the arrest, detention, abduction or any other form of deprivation of liberty by agents of the State or by persons or groups of persons acting with the authorization, support or acquiescence of the State, followed by a refusal to acknowledge the deprivation of liberty or by concealment of the fate or whereabouts of the disappeared person, which place such a person outside the protection of the law" (Article 2).

Forced disappearance is a crime against human rights when committed by a state agent or with the acquiescence of the State. It is a continuing offense since it begins with extrajudicial detention that denies access to families but does not prescribe until the person appears alive or dead. In human rights discourse, as in persecution and torture, a disappearance is not considered forced if it occurs in the domestic sphere or the public sphere if committed by private agents.

Today, Mexico challenges this definition since authorities of the State are not always directly involved, or at least not prominently or actively. In many cases, the degree of involvement of authorities is unknown since it may be through a network of corruption. It is this uncertainty that creates the grey area and related impunity, making forced disappearance a valuable tool in the necropolitical governmentalization of the State since the State can quickly distance itself from any responsibility when it appears to be the result of indiscriminate criminal violence that exonerates it from serious human rights violations. It is a strategy of necropower to create fear and avoid accountability regarding the deaths of men and women. The disappearance that follows the abduction or illegal detention of migrants, activists, uncomfortable politicians, journalists, or the victims of crime by criminals and authorities allows authorities to evade responsibility.

Concerning women, as we know from the figures for deaths and the principal place of women on search committees for the disappeared, in the war for control of the drugs market, the rates of death and disappearance are higher for men. The effects on women are mostly indirect (mothers, sisters, wives, sisters-in-law, daughters-in-law, and daughters). However, this does not mean that women are not murdered and disappeared. They are, but the violence associated with the war for the dispossession of women's bodies has another space-time dynamic formed by the nonsecuritized public sphere, the private or personal space, and a combination of the two, for domination and sexual exploitation.

The invisibility of women in the legal category of forced disappearance characterizes the no securitized public sphere. In legal terms, if a woman is a victim of rape, murder, and disappearance using chemical degradation, disposal in deep waters, or clandestine burial, it does not constitute forced disappearance but is simply a disappearance. The exception to this configuration of the crime of forced disappearance is in the Rome Statute of the International Criminal Court (ICC). The ICC recognizes as forced disappearance the disappearance of a person in the context of crimes against humanity, which include "rape, sexual slavery, forced prostitution, forced pregnancy, forced sterilization or other forms of sexual abuse of comparable gravity" when "committed as part of a widespread or systematic attack directed against any civilian population, with knowledge of the attack" (CPI 1998: Art. 7(1)(g)).

The justice system assumes the women reported as disappeared in reality "are there with their boyfriends" or ended up this way "due to their lifestyle," which connects them to spheres dominated by drug traffickers such as bars and brothels. The result is a convenient technology used to sell women's sexuality and enables a kind of patriarchy redux in narco-violence. For this reason, it is almost impossible to follow the trail of slavery and sexual and domestic violence in public and private spheres (Romero Malgarejo and Pech Matamoros 2014).

Studies of slavery for sexual exploitation have shown that traffickers "hook" their victims by first becoming devoted boyfriends; or fathers, mothers, and siblings use paralegal rules or appeal to tradition as a means to introduce them to prostitution, sell them or make them personal sex slaves. These young women then simply "disappear." For example, according to a study of pimps in the Náhuatl communities of Tlaxcala (Romero Malgarejo y Pech Matamoros 2014), men have been prostituting women since 1960. They have established a "school" where these pimps teach young men how to dress and speak to make young women from Oaxaca and Puebla, who work as carers or domestic workers in Mexico City, fall in love with them before forcing them into prostitution. As far as their families are concerned, they simply "disappeared" (Romero Malgarejo y Pech Matamoros 2014), but in reality, they are taken against their will and moved along a broad network of Tlaxcaltecan pimps in Mexico City, Guadalajara, Coatzacoalcos, Matamoros, Tampico, Tijuana, Tlaxcala, and Apizaco, in Mexico; and New York, Chicago, and Houston, in the United States.

Forced migration is critical in the forced disappearance of women because of two reasons. Firstly, traffickers usually work with smugglers, so their journey to prostitution spots across borders is a form of involuntary migration. Secondly, jobs available for women are in the sex trade. In order to dispossess women of their bodies, they make them their girlfriends, marry them, and even have children with them to persuade them not to escape. To dominate them, they brutally beat the women and their children, and even kill them, to keep them in slavery (Romero Malgarejo y Pech Matamoros 2014). While this happens, women's families believe they simply disappeared since they never hear from them again. In the context of systematically forced disappearance in Mexico, families assume girls and women disappeared in the same way that men did, in the circumstances linked to drug trafficking—instead of sexual violence and trafficking.

Massacres

The massacre is a standard lucrative death technology—the necropolitical technology *par excellence*. In conventional wars, concentration camps were central to the administration of life and death; in necropolitics, the technologies are more mobile (Mbembe 2011). The target populations of massacres are suspected employees of rival cartels; relatives of people from rival cartels; and people who are the direct object of revenge. As mentioned above, those who are somehow involved in drug violence—*sicarios* and their relatives—are at the same time poor, urban, violent, misogynistic, and disenfranchised males and their wives, children, and other relatives.

From 2006 to 2015, the media reported at least 13 massacres recorded, a count that does not exclude the possibility of others. The existence of 201 clandestine graves (2006–2015) suggests that disappearances may result from various murders and massacres (Open Society 2016). One of these massacres occurred at La Marquesa, Estado de México (2008), where 24 bricklayers were abducted and murdered by suspected members of La Familia Michoacana. In Acapulco, Guerrero (2010), an armed commando group abducted 22 tourists from Michoacán, 18 of whom appeared dead days later. In Villas de Salvárcar, Ciudad Juárez, Chihuahua (2010), suspected *sicarios* opened fire on 60 students aged 12 to 15, killing 16 and wounding 12. In Guadalajara, Jalisco (2011), suspected *narcos* dumped the bodies of 26 people at the Arcos del Milenio monument just a few days after the Pan American Games had commenced in the city. In Allende, Coahuila (2011), the Army burst into people's homes, set fire to businesses, and abducted 300 people who are still missing. In San Fernando, Tamaulipas (2011), 72 migrants were murdered by Los Zetas for refusing to work as sicarios.

Another massacre occurred in Monterrey, Nuevo León (2011; suspected members of Los Zetas burst into and set fire to a casino where they shot the owner for failing to pay protection; 52 people died in the fire. Also, armed men dumped 49 torsos along the stretch of a highway in Cadereyta, Nuevo León (2014), and the police and soldiers abducted and made disappear 43 students in Ayotzinapa, Guerrero (2014). In Tlatlaya, Estado de México (2014), the Army executed 22 alleged criminals who surrendered after detention. The same happened in Tahuato, Michoacán (2015), where the Federal Police executed 42 alleged criminals who had already surrendered. In Apatzingán, Michoacán (2015), the police and soldiers fired on self-defense groups, killing 16 and wounding 44. In Zitlala, an indigenous community in Guerrero (2015), an armed commando group murdered seven people. Finally, in Monterrey, Nuevo León (2016), inmates at the Topo Chico prison clashed in a bloody brawl that left 49 dead.

Feminicide

Regarding feminicide, it is "the misogynistic murder of women by men; it is a form of sexual violence" (Radford 2006: 33). However, what best defines feminicide in the Mexican case, is Julia Monárrez's (2009) concept of systematic sexual feminicide. This idea "includes or belongs to the totality of a system in which we find cultural, political, economic, and religious elements that converge to create the conditions for feminicide" (Monárrez Fragoso 2009: 2). These elements include social class, "skin color, the hegemony of patriarchal violence, capitalist violence, and illegalities" (Monárrez Fragoso 2009: 27).

Feminicide is used in the same way as extermination camps to implement the final solution to the Jewish question. Foucault stated that extermination camps were the most sophisticated biopolitical technologies used by the Nazis to kill Jews who had no scientific use or function as labor forces: women, children, and the old. In the war for the necropolitical dispossession of female bodies, the primary technology is feminicide. As with massacres, the intention is not extermination; what they do is kill those of no use, either because they resist sexual slavery for commercial purposes or due to the domination and self-affirmation of the Endriago subject (see chapter 1).

Endriagos not only seek recognition and wealth. They also seek self-affirmation by imposing their control over their woman, their children, and their homes. The Endriago can murder their partner or children or pay someone to do it if they discover they are straying from the private domain. They dominate through rape, control of fertility, control sexuality and economic autonomy, and abuse their children with impunity. Some women accede to the terms of Endriagos to protect their lives and those of their children or simply because they do not want to be alone because they have

CONCLUSION

In its production phase, the necropolitical apparatus of forced migration includes two strategies: *forced depopulation* and *lucrative death*. On the one hand, forced depopulation begins with extractivist projects facilitated by law enforcement officials, the military, organized crime, or a hybrid of a criminal with one or the other. These activities massively kill people but not without profit; that is why sex and organ trafficking, kidnapping, extortion, and smuggling are widespread. Those who survive lucrative death are displaced, internally or internationally, becoming forced migrants.

On the other hand, the contexts of lucrative death are a type of conflict that simultaneously explains criminal and sexual violence as part of a continuum of violence for securing criminal markets and commodifying women's bodies. Using Mexico as a case study, it describes two contexts of lucrative death: the war for the necropolitical governmentalization of the State and the dispossession of women's bodies. While these wars have different aims—co-opting and reconfiguring the State and dispossessing women of their bodies for commodification—they share a common feature: a dysfunctional, permanently corrupt, and deliberately deadly legal-spatial site that secures the impunity of their power technologies: massacre, feminicide, and forced disappearance. This necropolitics gives agents of war the control of drug markets and sex trafficking and slavery while subordinating women to the reproduction of the economy as a whole. Necropower produces forced migration through lucrative death-killings, massacres, disappearances, and feminicides functional to the illegal economy. Corporations depopulating resource-rich geographies may, in turn, buy Endriagos' death expertise.

The lives of those who survive the first two stages of the process are managed by legal and illegal technologies, such as smuggling and asylum systems that throw them to the margins of wealthy nations, as chapter 4 shall discuss. The forced migrant is the subject produced by the necropolitical apparatus of forced migration. The asylum regime produces the legal categories that allow for necropolitical management, as we shall see in chapter 3.

NOTE

1. Elsewhere, when discussing lucrative death in the context of the drug war, I called this necropolitical strategy "necropolitical wars" for the sake of argument. Necropolitical wars are helpful to understand lucrative death as part of a larger political strategy centered on the political subjectivity of the perpetrators of killings. Speaking about lucrative death directly as part of the ontology of the production of forced migration help us to focus on the subject position (see below) of forced migrants-to-be without focusing on the subjectivity of criminals as political actors. See: Estévez, Ariadna. 2019. "Necropolitical Wars." In Koram, Kojo. 2019. *The War on Drugs and the Global Colour Line*. London: Pluto Press. Estévez, Ariadna. 2018. *Guerras necropolíticas y biopolítica de asilo en América del Norte*. Mexico: CISAN/UNAM-UACM.

Chapter 3

From the Asylum Seeker to the Forced Migrant

Apparatuses produce subjects. The apparatus for the necropolitical production and management of forced migration *produces* forced migrants as a disposable subject. As a subject, the forced migrant is even more precarious than the *homo sacer* (Agamben 1998) because they live in permanent legal exception and because their death is productive and lucrative. Ultimately, capital accumulation through lucrative death cannibalizes forced migrants to exhaustion. However, there is nothing essential about it. The forced migrant is a subjectivity produced by a regime that has progressively tried to narrow down the scope of refugee law's international protection. This protection was already narrow as the result of colonial relations in international law.

Mayblin claims rightly that the core of the asylum regime, the 1951 Refugee Convention, was a colonial and racial project from its outset. It continues to be, as we can see in today's racialized, neocolonial, and necropolitical border regimes (Mayblin 2020a, 2020b, 2017). Furthermore, as Picozza points out, this is the coloniality of asylum: "(the) colonial sedimentations, particularly regarding contemporary manifestations of the category 'race,' (that) are rearticulated in the legal and social relations that refugees entertain with the 'host' society and its state" (Picozza 2021: 5).

The contemporary global governance of migration continues this colonial sedimentation and produces forced migrants for management purposes. Legally a refugee is a person who crosses borders seeking international protection in the event of political persecution. Asylum seekers become refugees and acquire related rights in the host country when they manage to prove before an asylum judge or official that the political authorities of their own country are unable or unwilling to protect them from persecution motivated by race or ethnicity, nationality, religion, political opinion, or belonging to a specific social group. In contrast, the forced migrant is not a legal category with neither related rights nor international protection. Forced migration is an emerging social and political category that policymakers use to name collectively and individually survivors of forced depopulation and lucrative death technologies.

The global governance of migration is the necropolitical apparatus of forced migration's governmentality—the institutional, legal, and discursive wrapping for the neoliberal management of mobility. The necropolitical apparatus of forced migration has gradually subsumed the international asylum and refugee regime, merging it with human rights law for management purposes. In its instrumental role within the apparatus, the asylum and refugee regime serve the rule of law necropower's *pro morituri* principle of establishing the lower possible protection standards for survivors of forced depopulation and lucrative death, producing them as disposable subjects. In global governance, "contemporary international law arranges political space and legal order" according to the "logic of the border" (Dehm 2020: 3).

The chapter draws attention to how global governance discourses have subsumed the asylum and refugee legal regime's instruments and laws to produce the forced migrant as the subject of the necropolitical management of mobility. It provides the classifications that allow the rule of law necropower to enforce *pro morituri* asylum laws and policies. To develop this argument, the chapter will first present a discussion of how global governance and its different regimes and technologies—the migration and human rights regimes—have become part of the necropolitical governmentality of the apparatus of forced migration. It develops short genealogies of the asylum regime and the refugee as a concept to show how the global governance of migration fragmented the legal category of the refugee and produced the forced migrant as a disposable nonlegal subject. The last section of the chapter describes how global governance further fragments forced migration into different policy categories according to the geographical boundaries and displacement causes for subsequent management purposes.

GLOBAL GOVERNANCE OF MIGRATION AS NECROPOLITICAL GOVERNMENTALITY

Globalization refers to the multiplicity of links and interconnections above and below the nation-state. Globalization is a process in which decisions and activities in one place of the world have consequences for individuals and communities in remote locations. There are constant flows of goods, people, capital, knowledge, culture, pollution, drugs, fashion, beliefs, and crime worldwide (Hernández Cervantes 2015). International scholars call *global governance* to the managerial and public policy discourse of globalization. Stoker (1998) argues that governance is different from a state's government.

The former is a governing style in which boundaries between the private and the public become blurred. Its institutions include state organizations as well as autonomous nongovernmental organizations—business-oriented and charities. Governance acknowledges ambiguity regarding public and private responsibilities for the solution of social and economic phenomena. It also encourages power and leadership-sharing between different actors (Stoker 1998).

Mezzadra and Nielsen (2013) point out that global governance is what Foucault called governmentality, the institutional rationality applying economic and managerial discourses and criteria to all kinds of social phenomena. For these authors, "The corporate language used to define these actors is far from neutral: it must be considered part and parcel of an attempt to spread the model, the language, and the rationality of the capitalist corporation throughout the whole fabric of global society and policies" (Mezzadra and Neilson 2013: 177). They go further, saying that for processing global phenomena from a managerial perspective, governmentality deploys fragmented and specialized areas of knowledge that, in turn, lead to the formation of epistemic and political communities. Groups of experts and politicians design and negotiate legal and policy strategies to regulate social phenomena-like migration. Together with the body of laws, institutions, and policies, epistemic and political communities inform "regimes" like the migration regime. For them, the migration regime's subject is the migrant worker, both as individual and collective.

Eduardo Domenech argues that the global governance of migration implies migration management with a worldwide approach. Policy in global migration management aims to regulate—instead of stopping—migration in an "orderly" way based on humanitarian and human rights discourses. Well-ordered migration's main objective is to prevent and stop "irregular" or "illegal" migration through the global articulation of the international community. Like any managerial approach, migration governance seeks to maximize benefits and advantages and minimize costs and risks. In the end, the global management of migration suggests "a division between 'desirable' and 'undesirable' migratory flows based on their orderly/disorderly, voluntary/forced and reduced/massive nature" that victimizes migrants and justifies border securitization (Domenech 2018: 112–113).

Mezzadra and Neilson agree with Domenech that human rights and humanitarian law are at the center of the global governance of migration to give the idea that it is "tough but humane" when it comes to border control and administration through securitization (Mezzadra and Neilson 2013: 175). Governmentality is analogous to governance, especially regarding issues such as the management of racism and migration because it allows regulating life and death in the name of human rights, liberty, and security. Bal Sokhi-Bulley

(2011) argues that human rights are government technologies guaranteeing a safe and secure society with the potential for regulation and normalization. The human rights perspective is essential in governmentality because it gives an impression of freedom while facilitating control (Sokhi-Bulley 2011: 256). When talking about the migration regime, Mezzadra and Neilson:

> refer, in the frame of our analysis of governance, to the contradictory and fragmentary formation of a body of knowledge within disparate epistemic and political communities. We further refer to the circulation at the global level of administrative techniques of control, technical standards, and capacity-building programs forged within these communities, which profoundly influence the formulation of migration policies and border control patterns. Governance presents itself within emerging border and migration regimes as a smooth process of persuasion without coercion according to neutral patterns of risk calculation and management, often emphasizing the "freedom of movement" of migrants (Mezzadra and Neilson 2013: 180).

Mezzadra and Neilson's view of the "migration regime" is not much different from Nicholas de Genova's (2010) "deportation regime." This author claims that since 9/11, there have been international efforts and cooperation for the externalization of border control that seeks to keep migrants off borders, chasing them, illegalizing them, and ultimately expelling and deporting them. For him, "The overall intent of such internationally coordinated mass deportation schemes is not only to remove 'illegal' migrants, 'suspect' refugees, and 'bogus' asylum seekers from their borders of the United States or Europe but to remove them from the borders of their borders, through the creation of an expanded buffer zone of graduated securitization" (De Genova 2010: 5).

Mezzadra and Neilson's "migration regime" and De Genova's "deportation regime" is the necropolitical apparatus of forced migration's governmentality. Here, asylum and refugee law and related human rights law are management technologies. Although Mezzadra and Neilson's migration regime is powerful—more comprehensive than De Genova's—they lack a more in-depth structural view beyond governance as labor management. Migration is not only managed but *produced.* Migration management's main objective is to administrate the subjective collateral damage of migration production strategies: forced migrants. However, Mezzadra and Neilson's appreciation of international human rights and humanitarian legal regimes helps to advance the argument that the categories these laws create exclude subjects that eventually become disposable. They claim that "contemporary systems of migration control and detention blur the borders between norm and exception, governance and sovereignty" and also "blur the borders between norm and exception, governance and sovereignty" (Mezzadra and Neilson 2013: 169).

Legal scholar Aleida Hernández Cervantes shares this view saying that in global governance, state sovereignty has changed and subordinated to an international legal regime that guarantees capital reproduction and neoliberal values through the primacy of the markets and the dispossession of lands and resources (Hernández Cervantes 2015). The overlapping of national and international law and policy facilitates the operation of neoliberal economics such as environmental degradation and land dispossession. It also regulates the social issues deriving from these activities, like migration and criminal and sexual violence. It is what Hernández Cervantes (2018) calls "legal structures of dispossession." These are the regulations operating as institutional mediations for dispossession and occur both at the international headquarters of global economic powers and national office through the form of transnational legal production (Hernández Cervantes 2018: 47).

What the international community used to call the asylum regime has disappeared. As such, the migration regime subsumed it within the humanitarian and human rights legal apparatus. The asylum and refugee regime became necropolitical governmentality's power technology for migration management. As explained in chapter 2, the necropolitical apparatus of forced migration produces migration through a series of laws and policies aimed at depopulating geographies rich in natural resources using criminal, state, and gender violence; survivors flee seeking refuge in other countries. The apparatus administrates forced displacement through migration and asylum laws, ultimately dumping in the third world the deported and those who were refused entrance to destination rich countries. As a necropolitical technology, the legal category of asylum in human rights and humanitarian law becomes a legitimate way of excluding all those who fail to conform to its core definition.

The asylum seeker is almost the only form left of documented or legal migration for people fleeing political, criminal, economic, environmental, and cultural hardship and discrimination. For this reason, fascist or at least right-wing regimes such as Donald Trump's in the US (2017–2021) and recently approved international laws and policies—the Marrakesh Pacts of 2018—follow the necropolitical *pro morituri* principle, replacing the "refugee" with such terms as "forced migration," "convention refugees," "mix fluxes" and other categories that give no rights to people. As immunization (Esposito 2005), the asylum category makes sure that forced depopulation survivors become disposable subjects in the necropolitical apparatus of forced migration. According to Dehm (2020: 9), international law authorizes state violence toward refugees, which results "in practices of border control of refugees themselves as a form of exclusion and deterrence." In what remains of chapter 3, the author addresses two interconnected genealogical problematizations: how the legal categories and concepts used in this regime and its related epistemic communities derived in what we know today as the forced migrant, and how the International Refugee Regime became absorbed by the necropolitical apparatus of forced migration.

LEGAL CATEGORIES PRODUCING NECROPOLITICAL SUBJECTIVITIES: FROM THE REFUGEE TO THE FORCED MIGRANT

In legal terms, the refugee is the status that international law grants to forced migrants who cross borders seeking international protection in the event of political persecution. The 1951 Convention Relating to the Status of Refugees and its 1967 Protocol provides the refugee's core international definition (Article 1(A2)). It defines a refugee as a person who:

> 2. As a result of events occurring before 1 January 1951 and owing to a well-founded fear of being persecuted for reasons of race, religion, nationality, membership of a particular social group, or political opinion, is outside the country of his nationality and is unable or, owing to such fear, is unwilling to avail himself of the protection of that country; or who, not having a nationality and being outside the country of his former habitual residence as a result of such events, is unable or, owing to such fear, is unwilling to return to it.

According to the United Nations High Commissioner for Refugees (UNHCR), refugee status is declaratory. Therefore, any person who qualifies as a refugee is, by that very fact, a refugee, regardless of the formal recognition of the host country. However, in a world where sovereignty is crucial, the reality is a far cry from UN idealism, and asylum seekers become refugees acquiring related rights in the host country when they can prove persecution before an asylum judge or official. Claimants have to demonstrate that political authorities in their own country are unable or unwilling to protect them from persecution based on race or ethnicity, nationality, religion, political opinion, or belonging to a specific social group. However, the international asylum and refugee regime fails to automatically protect forced migrants produced by the political economy, global development, criminal violence, environmental degradation, and general forms of forced depopulation and lucrative death. The international community designed the asylum and refugee regime to respond to a specific political context, and today necropowers instrumentalize these historical boundaries to exclude most forced migrants.

Violence and the political economy are no new concepts. However, many of their contemporary expressions—generalized criminal violence, drugs/humans trafficking, and climate change, for example—fall outside the parameters of core legal instruments and the mandate of specialized multilateral organizations. Furthermore, the "forced migrant" is not a legal category with related rights or international protection. Forced migration became a social and political term for people who leave their countries for a reason other than economic necessity or persecution; the former is a so-called economic migrant and the latter an "asylum seeker" who may apply for refugee status.

Determining who qualifies as a refugee—a person worthy of international protection—is an essentially political decision made by nation-states. Ortega-Velázquez (2019) claims that even though states ratifying or adhering to an international treaty have binding legal obligations, state sovereignty still plays a primary role in international law, regardless of the human rights issues involved in individual claims. For this reason, international instruments of the universal system, which are the current basis of the legal protection system for refugees, do not impose on the signatory states the obligation to grant refugee status to each person who requests asylum, and they have the freedom to establish their own rules, procedures, and institutions to process asylum applications and make decisions. In this way, she claims, more than a human right, asylum is a "state prerogative" (Ortega Velázquez 2019: 75).

Certain countries—in particular, hegemonic and colonial powers—frequently use refugee status to punish, harass, or pressure their political and economic enemies. For example, from 1966 to 2017, as part of the Cuban Adjustment Act, the US famously granted immediate asylum to Cuban and Chinese citizens, mostly activists, to punish communist regimes (Ramji-Nogales, Schoenholtz, and Schrag 2008). Another example is the Venezuelans displaced abroad. By 2019 there were 3.6 million Venezuelan refugees in the world. There were twice as many Syrian refugees (6.6 million), but the UNCHR singles out Venezuela in its 2019 report saying that around the globe there were "26.0 million refugees, 20.4 million refugees, under UNHCR's mandate, 5.6 million Palestine refugees under UNRWA's mandate, 45.7 million internally displaced people, 4.2 million asylum seekers and 3.6 million Venezuelans displaced abroad" (UNHCR 2020: 2). It would seem that Venezuela surpassed Syria or even Palestine. Today, Venezuela is a gold mining hot spot, and president Nicolás Maduro is excluding the US from it—see the book's introduction and chapter 3. Singling out Venezuela has no empirical justification. It is political.

Nevertheless, international law has marked the scope of this political decision. The UN has argued that states should not use sovereignty as an excuse to refuse legal protection to people suffering from persecution and other threats, although in practice, it often is. For instance, in 2017, the Trump administration abandoned negotiations for the Global Compact for Safe, Regular, and Orderly Migration. Nikki Haley, the American envoy to the UN General

Assembly, claimed the global management of refugees and migration was a "subversion of American sovereignty" (Wintour 2017). In 2018, during his annual address to the UN General Assembly, president Donald Trump stated that global governance and trade were contrary to the interests of American sovereignty, especially concerning such issues as migration and the environment (Terminski 2018).

Black (2001) believes that from the very beginning, the term "refugee" was enshrined in law and produced for policy purposes, without any critical content. Today, "refugee" does not describe the social, political, and economic conditions of a subject seeking refuge, but prescribes a series of legal requirements, the burden of proof for someone claiming asylum (Black 2001). The definition of the refugee in the International Regime lacks critical content. It refers exclusively to people who fled their countries before 1951; the time frame does not describe a condition—that of the refugee—but a time limit for legal and policy purposes. Baker and Polzer believe the lack of analytical content in the term "refugee" makes people invisible and privileges policy-makers' worldviews who are often guided by political agendas (Bakewell 2008, Polzer 2008).

Persecution as a critical component of the legal—as opposed to normative—definition of the refugee seems to be part of the problem for scholars supporting the so-called humanitarian view of persecution in the right to asylum (Coles 1989, Carens 2013, Shacknove 1985, Zolberg 1983). Others, though, believe persecution is the only possible way to distinguish economic from forced migrants; these scholars support a so-called political view of persecution (Hathaway 2005, Price 2006). Generally speaking, the asylum law defines the fear of persecution as fear of severe harm and the state's failure to provide protection *vis a vis* this possibility. Persecution is, therefore, a sustained and systematic human rights abuses indicating the state's failure to protect and in which the level of harm must be severe. In order to demonstrate persecution, a person's experience must be more than simple unpleasantness, harassment, or even essential suffering. Scholars believe that persecution as a fundamental part of the refugee definition excludes many of the contemporary refugees.

On the one hand, among scholars supporting humanitarian views of persecution, we find Gervase Coles, who believes that diplomats devised the persecution criterion to address a particular problem in a particular time (the refugees of World War II in Europe). They did not mean to do it normative or for general application (Coles 1989). Joseph Carens claims that contemporary international politics is concerned with constraining refugee status rather than giving protection on a moral basis because the causes should be irrelevant vis a vis the moral obligation to protect (Carens 2013). Andrew Shacknove claims that a refugee should be the person whose basic needs or human rights are unprotected by their country and have no choice but to seek international protection. Generalized political, criminal, or gender violence are severe forms of harm and, therefore, should be considered forms of persecution in the sense of the 1951 Convention (Shacknove 1985). Aristide Zolberg argues that today, asylum seekers include three types: political activists, targets of genocide, and victims of generalized violence, and policy and law should change accordingly (Zolberg 1983).

On the other hand, scholars supporting political asylum include James Hathaway, who argues that refugee status must be given based on a broad interpretation of serious harm, the underlying criterion in persecution. The persecution criterion is not arbitrary but a way to choose "the most deserving among the deserving" in migratory flows. They are unlikely to find protection in their home country because they are politically excluded (Hathaway 2005). Matthew Price claims that other forced migrants could do with temporary protection *vis a vis* disaster, generalized violence, or famine; asylum seekers need a new political membership or citizenship. Political asylum based on persecution is a way of morally condemning a repressive regime. He claims that keeping persecution as the basis for an asylum claim does not prevent other refugees from getting international protection, but other categories should be used, that is, temporary protection, military intervention, and resettlement programs. Persecution on the grounds of religion, nationality, ethnicity, political opinion, and the particular group makes an argument about the state's legitimate use of the means of coercion (Price 2006).

Indian legal scholar Bhupinder S. Chimni agrees with the political view of persecution but from a critical rather than supportive viewpoint. Being a postcolonial jurist—a member of the Harvard-based Third World Approaches to International Law (TWAIL)—Chimni believes that states have always used the refugee legal category for political purposes—along with the four phases of its evolution (Chimni 2009). During the first phase (1914–1945), when the international community witnessed the fall of the Ottoman and Habsburg empires, World War I, and the Armenian genocide, the incipient Refugee Regime was led by practical interests, such as attracting professional refugees, including medical doctors and scientists. The second phase (1945–1982) was marked by the political interests of the West in the immediate post-World War II period (the split between capitalist and socialist countries), and Cold War politics (dissidents in one bloc or the other). The third phase (1980–2000) was marked by the proliferation of countries producing refugees in the Third World due to military *coups d' état* and interventions sponsored by Western democracies (Chimni 1998, Chimni 2009). The civil war in Guatemala is an excellent example of how Western military intervention led to an exodus of thousands of people. After a twenty-year civil war, Guatemalan General Efraín Ríos Montt took power in 1982, enforcing counterinsurgency operations to eliminate guerrillas and opposition groups. As a result, the conflict displaced internally one million indigenous people (of Mayan descent) and sent into exile to Mexico other 200,000. Only a quarter of these refugees remained in UNHCR camps (Jonas 2013). The fourth and final period corresponds to the current post-9/11 era, marked by the threat of terrorism, criminal violence, and the intensification of climate change. Internal and international forced migration has continued to increase in this period. Forced migration studies appeared and evolved during the last two periods. It first emerged in the 1980s, when people started to flee their home countries for reasons other than political persecution, which is the cornerstone of the international refugee regime. Since then, forced migration has become a critical category in policy (Chimni 2009, Chimni 1998).

A focus on refugees as part of the broader topic of migration studies only emerged in the context of an increase in refugee numbers. Zetter (2007) argues that the proliferation of causes and the increase in figures led to a *fractioning* of the refugee label within forced migration studies. There was a multiplication of related labels used to manage intense migration flows and increasingly exclude more people from the legal protection of refugee status. These labels are referred to in this chapter as "types of forced migration"—see the next section. Zetter regrets this shift from refugee studies to forced migration studies since it has negative consequences for policy given that the refugee regime allowed for real protection from persecution. He claims that globalization is reshaping the refugee regime and, therefore, the concept of the refugee itself since the original objective of determining how humanitarian assistance was distributed and accessed was replaced by an interest in distinguishing who is and who is not a refugee (Zetter 2007: 174). The politics of international protection is no longer focused on state obligation but on restricting refugee status according to who is considered a desirable migrant and who is not (Squire 2009: 7). Discussing voluntary/involuntary migration, or forced migration, is a form of *fractioning* the refugee label, and some scholars seek to ground these new labels in human rights law and rhetoric, for both analytical and policy objectives.

SUBSUMING THE INTERNATIONAL LEGAL REFUGEE REGIME

Dehm claims there is an entanglement of international law and "the colonial histories of necropolitical spaces that inform contemporary state border regimes" (Dehm 2020: 3). The institutional and law development of the International Refugee Regime confirms this hypothesis. The regime started as a response to displacement in Europe. It worked as expected until displacement was no longer a European issue affecting mostly white males. When the regime seemed to provide relief for people from the third world, the migration regime absorbed its institutional and legal frameworks and made it a managerial structure for the necropolitical apparatus of forced migration. This section traces back the institutional and legal development of the refugee regime, from its beginning to its subsumption.

Institutional Subsumption

The international refugee regime was established in the early twentieth century by the League of Nations, which founded the High Commission for Refugees, the first organization designed to address displacement caused by the Russian Revolution, World War I, and the disintegration of the Ottoman and Habsburg empires (Martin 2010). Several other offices replaced the Commission until the modern UNHCR was established in 1950 to deal with mass displacement from communist countries (Martin 2010). Betts claims that in its early years, the UNHCR was an isolated organization, but eventually became the core of a complex system of international institutions overlapping with other bodies dealing with human rights and mobility within the UN and regional multilateral institutions (Betts 2010). Two of them are essential because they widened up the scope of the UN's definition. Firstly, the Organization of African Unity (OAU) issued in 1969 the Convention Governing the Specific Aspects of Refugee Problems in Africa, which extended the UN definition to include targeted not only persecution but also people who are simply "compelled" to leave their country. Secondly, in Latin America, in the context of the Organization of American States (OAS), experts drafted the 1984 Cartagena Declaration on Refugees, a nonbinding document that further extended the definition to the threat to life, security and freedom in the context of generalized violence. For policy and legal purposes, the European Union (EU) and the Asian-African Legal Consultative Organization (AALCO) adopt the UN's definition of the refugee; their human rights instruments do not include the right to asylum, unlike OAS and OAU. However, in 2004 the EU issued a Directive establishing temporary "subsidiary protection" for people who is not a Convention refugee but would face a real risk of suffering serious harm if returned to their country.

Until very recently, the asylum regime was separate from the human rights universal system. The UN human rights institutions dealt with the rights of migrant workers and their families but not asylum. The UN Office of the High Commissioner for Human Rights, the Human Rights Council, and the Council's Special Rapporteur on the Human Rights of Migrants do not deal with forced migration. However, if necessary, the universal human rights system appeals to the 1951 Convention and its 1967 Protocol. It can only consider the Convention on the Reduction of Statelessness, the Convention Relating to the Status of Stateless Persons, and the Declaration on The Human Rights of Individuals Who Are Not Nationals of The Country In Which They Live. From 2001 onwards, human rights legislation provides criteria for complementary means of protection for refugees. Merging both systems is not as good as it sounds, as the section below will discuss.

Law Subsumption

In 1951 the UN issued the Convention Relating to the Status of Refugees. Neither the Convention nor its 1967 Protocol, which removed the Convention's temporal limitation, imposed on States the obligation to grant refugee status to every person claiming asylum. That was not the only colonial bias of the Convention, in any case. Only the 1969 Convention Governing the Specific Aspects of Refugee Problems in Africa and the 1984 Cartagena Declaration on Refugees consider generalized violence as a valid cause for seeking asylum; the Convention does not. The Convention, however, establishes persecution as the leading cause for asylum; eventually, persecution as the core criterion for granting refugee status has become problematic because of the complexities of the phenomenon.

The refugee Convention neither included gender considerations nor women's experiences of violence. The Convention excluded specific forms of persecution suffered by women in the home country. It also excludes women who suffer from gender-based violence as a specific social group from the outset. Although sex is considered an acceptable immutable feature, it is not enough to prove visibility and particularity because domestic violence occurs in the home. This group could be considered too broad in countries with misogynistic legal, social, and political systems. It even excludes women who are the victims of criminal gang violence. However, in 1995 the UN corrected this omission by issuing gender guidelines for assessing sexual violence-based persecution. In 2002 the UN issued new standards, the Guidelines on International Protection: Gender-Related Persecution within the context of Article 1A(2) of the 1951 Convention and its 1967 Protocol. These Guidelines state that while perpetrators of persecution are mostly state agents, in the case of discrimination and sexual and gender violence, perpetrators could be non-state actors often tolerated by the state.

Almost seventy years after the regime was established, and with multiplying refugee crises around the world, international policy and law are failing to broaden the scope of protection for refugee status. Recent legal and policy changes seem to confirm the scholarly hypothesis that "fractioning" the term refugee (Zetter 2007) serves the racist objective of keeping third-world nationals out of rich countries since nine out of ten refugees live in poor countries. The European Union (EU) is a right—or terrible—example of this. For policy and legal purposes, the EU adopts the UN definition for the refugee since its regional instruments do not include the right to seek asylum. This failure to recognize asylum at the regional level has allowed fascist groups and parties to impose their views on the Union's approach to the issue. In 2004 the EU issued a Directive establishing temporary "subsidiary protection" for people who are not Convention refugees but would face a real risk of suffering serious harm if returned to their country. Nevertheless, the EU's response to ever-increasing refugee "crises" in its areas of influence—Asia and Africa—is becoming increasingly repressive, with a series of measures intended to prevent third-country nationals from entering the Schengen Area. These measures include removing legal alternatives for reaching Europe (i.e., overseas embassies no longer accept asylum claims), preventing ships from setting sail for Europe and imposing penalties on transport companies that allow people to travel without documents.

The EU's racist approach to migration and refugees became institutionalized with the Dublin III Regulation, which entered into force in 2014 and builds on the Dublin Convention of 1990, or Regulation I, and the Dublin II Regulation, of 2003. The Regulation requires asylum seekers to request asylum in the first European nation they arrive in, preventing them from choosing the country they wish to go to, and which is often determined by colonial ties, previous migration, family networks, and cultural affinity. In addition to placing most of the burden on border countries—usually Greece and Italy—the regulation is inefficient since it clogs the asylum claim processing system. Sadly, racist institutional approaches to asylum help determine European attitudes towards migrants and asylum seekers, with Brexit being an excellent example of this. European refugee policy has also generated a backlash of populist anti-immigrant parties.

Institutionalized racism towards migrants and asylum seekers is becoming an international trend, taking over the UN system, as shown by the process for the adoption of the Global Compact for Safe, Orderly, and Regular Migration and the Global Compact on Refugees, a process starting in 2001. To mark the fiftieth anniversary of the Refugee Convention, and due to the increasing number of refugees and the multiplication of causes leading to national and international forced displacement, the UNHCR called for Global Consultations on International Refugee Protection (2001). This process led to the UNHCR issuing guidelines that recommended governments define "refugee" in a broader sense and use protection mechanisms in addition to those of the 1951 Convention, also known as "Complementary Protection." Complementary protection covers "Non-Convention-Refugees" who receive "Non-Convention Protection," which includes UN General Assembly resolutions and also regional declarations, conventions, and jurisprudence that allegedly expand the definition of the refugee and the scope of protection. Also, complementary protection includes human rights and humanitarian law, helping to support non-refoulment measures. Crucial means of complementary protection are universal and regional human rights instruments prohibiting torture, such as the 1984 UN Convention against Torture and Other Cruel, Inhuman or Degrading Treatment or Punishment (CAT), the European Convention on Human Rights (EHCR), the Inter-American Convention on Human Rights (1969), and the African Charter on Human and Peoples' Rights (1986). Under human rights law prohibiting torture, people whose cases fall outside the mandate of the 1951 Convention—they are not persecuted because of their nationality, ethnicity, political opinion, or belonging to a group—would be protected from deportation claiming a well-founded fear of being tortured, ill-treated or punished if returning to their country.

A liberal reading of "complementary protection" would indicate that making human rights laws complementary protection for refugees is an improvement. However, following the arguments of Mezzadra and Nielson (2013) and Sokhi-Bulley (2011) discussed in the first section of the chapter, human rights are technologies of power intended to give the impression that policy is humane despite its grounding in security and racist discourses. As Sokhi-Bulley claims:

> This perspective on rights is thus important because of what it tells us about the nature of rights discourse—that rights are technologies of governmentality, meaning that rights discourse governs and that we accept that government. Furthermore, we do it with a (false) sense of being liberated and less governed, we do it not knowing how that governmentality operates. This is significant since it not only disturbs but inverts the liberal tradition of rights—of rights against the state, or against government. Moreover, we in fact govern ourselves, becoming (lay)experts in our own right. The strength of a governmentality of rights model is that it is reflexive: rights act as tactics which link the "values" that they represent with our own desires (Sokhi-Bulley 2011: 256).

Making human rights institutions and legislation complementary to the legal and institutional instruments of the refugee regime seemed a measure guided by the *pro persona* principle of international law. Instead, it was a decision based on the necropolitical legal *pro morituri* principle. *Pro morituri* is the necropolitical antithesis of *the pro persona* principle, which means an interpretation of the law that criminalizes and punishes migration or narrows down international protection for refugees—see chapter 1. Merging asylum and human rights laws gave justification to the rule of law necropowers for controlling migration regulation in the necropolitical apparatus. Merging both asylum and human rights laws legitimizes the *pro morituri* legal choice of dismissing the need to widen up the scope of binding laws—expanding the refugee definition beyond the Convention and its Protocol.

Also, merging asylum and refugee laws with human rights treaties reinforced the problems that contemporary asylum seekers must prove before migration courts and offices that their case fits within the core definitions of persecution and protected groups—definitions demanding the claimant to prove that state officials instead of criminals or corporations are involved in human rights abuses. The author discussed elsewhere (Estévez 2013) that human rights, as a discourse, have truth effects: they establish subjectivities, objects, and concepts that divide the false from the true. In order to create these truth effects, human rights rely on other true discourses such as law and criminology. Human rights have truth effects over what constitutes a violation of physical integrity and life, a victim, and a context of widespread abuse. Human rights discourse has constructed a truth regime in which the definition of state attribution, responsibility, victim, and context excludes many subjectivities, objects, and concepts derived from contemporary necropolitical relations of domination, such as those of forced depopulation and lucrative death. Human rights construct *true* narratives in which state actors are always the main perpetrators and are responsible for human rights violations such as executions, forced disappearances, and persecution. However, the hybrid character of forced depopulation and lucrative death subvert the politics of truth in human rights discourse because it relies on the philosophical assumption of an alleged division between the public and the private—typical of liberal legal systems—that in necropolitics becomes even more blurred.[1] Consequently, extending refugee protection to include core human rights treaties reinforced already existing limitations.

Shortly after, the New York Declaration for Refugees and Migrants (2015) institutionalized the *pro morituri* principle of the asylum and human rights regimes merge. As a result of the consultation process and adoption of the 2030 Agenda for Sustainable Development in 2015, the UN General Assembly adopted the New York Declaration. In this Declaration, state parties "invite the private sector and civil society, including refugee and migrant organizations, to participate in multi-stakeholder alliances to support efforts to implement the commitments we are making today" (Preamble, 15). The Declaration shifts the regime's focus from state responsibility to the cooperation of Non-State Actors. Also, while emphasizing the UN commitment to human rights, the Declaration calls for a policy designed to prevent refugees from fleeing or seeking asylum in rich countries. It calls to "ease pressure on host countries; enhance refugee self-reliance; expand access to third-country solutions; support conditions in countries of origin for return." While the Declaration allegedly intended to tackle the shortcomings of hardcore refugee laws, it called on governments and civil society to work together while trying to prevent refugees from reaching rich countries rather than doing anything to save lives. In turn, the Declaration legitimized the so-called safe third country treaties, which allow the rule of law necropowers to use third-world border neighbor countries as massive, open-air detention centers that eventually become tools for management technologies within the necropolitical apparatus of forced migration. These treaties legalize non-refoulment measures (Ortega Velázquez 2017).

The Global Compact for Safe, Orderly and Regular Migration, and the Global Compact on Refugees reinforced the Declaration's necropolitical perspective. Both were adopted in December 2018. The goal of these non-binding instruments is to prevent asylum seekers and migrants from reaching the West. Third world countries are requested to receive asylum seekers; in exchange, rich countries and the private sector invest in services and infrastructure—third safe country agreements. There is no indication of how the international community will share this responsibility regarding the economic, political, and ethnic roots of forced depopulation, such as climate change, development projects, and crime. Rich countries will only accept refugees and undocumented migrants through "legal" and limited means such as family reunification, student scholarships, or humanitarian visas.

Human rights complementary protection, the New York Declaration, and the Marrakesh Pacts were the corollary of the institutional and law subsumption of the asylum regime in the necropolitical apparatus of forced migration, legitimizing the fragmentation of the refugee legal category.

Fractioning the Refugee

The rise of the forced migration policy category and the institutional and legal merging of the human rights and asylum regimes legitimized the refugee's fractioning. Policy and legal discourses of migration establish two basic types of migration: voluntary and forced. Voluntary migration implies a voluntary decision usually based on economic calculations—the subject seeking better opportunities abroad. In contrast, forced migration, also known as displacement, implies the subject's involuntary response to existing political, environmental, and violence-related threats (Reed, Ludwig, and Braslow 2016). For policy purposes, the UN defines forced migration as the "migratory movement in which an element of coercion exists, including threats to life and livelihood, whether arising from natural or man-made causes" (IOM in Reed Ludwig, and Braslow 2016: 605). Policymakers classify forced migrants according to geographical boundaries and the causes of displacement. This classification has implications for both policy and protection.

In the first place, the classification according to geographical boundaries includes asylum seekers, refugees, people in refugee-like situations, internally displaced persons (IDPs), and groups of people of concern. Firstly, asylum seekers are individuals who cross international borders seeking protection, but whose claim for refugee status is still pending. Asylum seekers such as those arriving in Australia by boat, or people who claim asylum in the United States while not holding a valid visa, are often detained in prison-like centers. Secondly, refugees are asylum seekers who have proved before a judge or immigration officer (depending on the country) a well-founded fear of persecution to receive refugee status under the terms of the Convention Relating to the Status of Refugees, its 1967 Protocol, the African Convention, and the UNHCR Statute. Even though States do not have an obligation to grant asylum or admit refugees, they do have the obligation not to forcibly return asylum seekers to the countries where they are facing persecution—the right to *non-refoulment*. States may relocate people in countries where they are safe, and states are willing to accept them. These are known as safe third countries. The Convention allows States to establish their terms to admit refugees.

Some countries have a very narrow interpretation of the Convention and grant asylum to people who have a well-founded fear of persecution based only on the five protected categories and if the state is unwilling or incapable of protecting them. Asylum seekers who are granted refugee status by a sovereign state according to the Convention have several rights that other forced migrants do not, including the same civil rights and liberties as citizens, the right to work, and access to social services for them and their children (including education and health). In some countries, refugees may become citizens, such as New Zealand, Canada, and Australia.

Thirdly, people in refugee-like situations are "groups of persons who are outside their country or territory of origin and who face protection risks similar to those of refugees, but for whom refugee status has, for practical or other reasons, not been ascertained" (UNHCR 2013). People in refugee-like situations include stateless persons and those denied protection in their own country, like the Bidoon in Kuwait and the Rohingya in Myanmar.

Fourthly, internally displaced persons (IDPs). In 1998, the UN issued the Guiding Principles on Internal Displacement, which define IDPs as "persons or groups of persons who have been forced or obliged to flee or to leave their homes or places of habitual residence, in particular as a result of, or in order to, avoid the effects of armed conflict, situations of generalized violence, violations of human rights or natural or human-made disasters, and who have not crossed an internationally recognized State border" (UN Commision on Human Rights 1998). IDPs remain within their home country and have the same rights and duties as other citizens. For example, they enjoy the right to health but are also responsible before the law if they commit crimes. More importantly, IDPs have the right to enjoy civil liberties and receive humanitarian aid, especially women, children, and the elderly. The Guidelines recommend governments to ban "arbitrary" displacement affecting indigenous peoples such as that caused by war and conflict. It should be noted that the ban does not include displacement related to environmental devastation and development projects. However, governments are called upon to protect peasants and indigenous people in cases where development projects evict local communities. Finally, groups or people of concern include refugees and IDPs who have returned to their home countries spontaneously or in an "organized fashion" that guarantees safety and dignity, with the help of the UNHCR (UNHCR 2018). People of concern include persons who were denied asylum and needed humanitarian assistance.

In the second place, classification according to the causes includes five types of forced migration as determined by the causes of displacement: conflict-induced, environmental or natural disaster-induced, development-induced, human trafficking, and mixed migration. First, conflict-induced displacement is the typical kind of forced migration, since it is displacement (national or international) caused by international or civil war or other political or social processes that lead to persecution under the categories protected by the 1951 Convention. Most UNHCR efforts concentrate on this type of displacement, which produces the type of refugee protected under the 1951 Convention. However, in new types of conflict such as lucrative death (that often entail widespread sexual violence against women), the terms of refugee status according to international law may be insufficient. In such cases, individuals do not belong to any of the Convention's five protected categories, and migration authorities dismiss it as "generalized violence." The Cartagena Declaration considers generalized violence a valid justification for claiming asylum, but it is not a binding document.

An example of this type of conflict is the case of Mexico, where drug cartels and law enforcement officials sometimes collude in cases of forced disappearance, kidnapping, execution, torture, persecution, femicide, rape, and massacres—what chapter 2 called lucrative death. While the government claims criminal gangs are solely responsible for these brutalities, and it invests essential resources in security as well as in judicial and Constitutional reform, among other normative changes, it has failed to tackle impunity and corruption. Even though the Mexican government claims to have taken measures to combat these crimes, they continue to occur. As a consequence, by 2018, there were 329,917 people internally displaced in 25 violent episodes, with 60 percent of this number represented by women and 92 percent by families (CMDPDH 2018). As for asylum seekers, from 2006 to 2016, Mexicans seeking asylum summed up 111,176, as discussed in chapter 2.

In recent years, criminal, gang, and sexual violence have become so severe and widespread in some regions that they have led to humanitarian crises and large-scale national and international displacement. Those who flee conflict or generalized violence could be "specially" designated refugees by the UN High Commissioner for Refugees (Martin 2010), or as part of geographically specific legal instruments like the African Convention and the Cartagena Declaration. Policy for refugees recognized by the UNHCR in these terms aims to address a temporary crisis since it is considered an emergency movement of people placed in temporary camps. However, after years of displacement, these camps develop into cities, with economic activities dependent on international aid. One such example is the Kakuma camp in Kenya, established in 1992, for people fleeing the war in Sudan. By 2017, it held over 164,000 people, that is, a population slightly larger than that of Curacao Island (160,000). There is a local paper-based economy since people live on vouchers that they exchange for access to schools and meals, among other things (Anzilotti 2017). When crises are over, people return to their homes, although sometimes the seriousness of the crisis leads to resettlement. For example, Hartisheik camp—located in Eastern Ethiopia—closed in 2004 after its 230,000 refugee population returned to Somalia, where an ongoing civil war had expelled thousands of people since 1988 (Healy and Bradbury 2010).

Second, environmental or natural disaster-induced migration includes the forced mobility of people affected by natural or human-made disasters related to climate change, environmental degradation, and other natural forces such as hurricanes, floods, earthquakes, and drought. By 2017, there were 18.8 million people internally displaced in 135 countries as a consequence of natural disasters. The most affected nations are in Asia, the Caribbean, and, more disproportionately, small Pacific islands (Small Island Developing States, SIDS). There is no specific legal protection for people who cross international borders fleeing human-caused environmental problems (climate change, disasters, degradation). Protection for "environmental refugees" depends upon sovereign states, who have no binding obligations to take them in or to grant them fundamental rights. For example, in 2017, the Immigration and Protection Tribunal of New Zealand ruled against two families from Tuvalu, a 2.5-square kilometer SIDS in the Pacific, who claimed protection under the 1951 Convention because the island's exposure to rising sea levels and storms makes life unsustainable (Bonnett 2017).

Third, there is development-induced forced migration. According to Reed, Ludwig, and Braslow (2016), economic development projects are the most critical cause of displacement in the contemporary world, even though the UNHCR focuses on conflict-displacement. Projects include population redistribution, urban development, mining, dams, irrigation schemes, transport, expansion of agricultural areas, and even conservation projects. These are often funded by the World Bank but also by corporations. In this type of displacement, forced mobility is the result of land and territory becoming contested spaces, leading to evictions, and the loss of property, jobs, shelter, and even their sense of community. The international community justifies this type of development in terms of economic progress (Terminski 2012). Between 2004 and 2013, 7,200 World Bank development projects displaced 3.4 million people; 97 percent of them were in Africa, Vietnam, China, and India (Chavkin et al. 2015). In India, 388,794 people have been displaced by twenty-four projects alone; one of these projects is the coal-power Tata Mundra Ultra Mega Power Project in Gujarat state, where entire fishing communities have lost their main economic activity as a result of the plant's heated wastewater (Yeoman 2015). In Honduras, where thousands of people fled the country in late 2018 as an immediate consequence of rampant and widespread violence, a palm oil producer and World Bank Group—sponsored Dinant is suspected of ordering its private guards to kill a local activist and preacher, Gregorio Chávez. They complained against the corporation that was disputing land ownership with a farming community in Panama Village. Another 132 activists have been killed in a civil war between farmers and corporations disputing land. The Honduras case shows that development-induced displacement also occurs in the form of conflict and violence generated by corporate interests (Chavkin 2015).

Fourth, human trafficking. According to the United Nations Trafficking in Persons Protocol (Article 3, Paragraph a), trafficking:

> shall mean the recruitment, transportation, transfer, harboring or receipt of persons, by means of the threat or use of force or other forms of coercion, of abduction, of fraud, of deception, of the abuse of power or of a position of vulnerability or of the giving or receiving of payments or benefits to achieve the consent of a person having control over another person, for the purpose of exploitation. Exploitation shall include, at a minimum, the exploitation of the prostitution of others or other forms of sexual exploitation, forced labour or services, slavery or practices similar to slavery, servitude or the removal of organs.

It is evident in the "transfer" and the use of "force" for exploitation purposes. Victims of trafficking are not merely displaced and may claim asylum because they belong to a particular social group and face persecution for this reason (Andersen 2014). Sexual trafficking victimizes mostly women and children, who are exploited in developed countries where consumers are often males from the developed world (sex tourism). For example, Dubai is known as the capital of human trafficking, with over 100,000 people trafficked into the country every year. Traffickers lure their victims from Asia and Africa from their home countries with the promise of jobs as domestic servants. Once they are in Dubai, criminals retain their passports and force them to work as prostitutes or domestic servants in conditions of slavery and sexual and physical abuse (Boycott UAE Team 2017).

Fifth and last, mixed migration refers to the flux of voluntary and involuntary migrants who take the same routes to the same destinations (Mix Migration Hub 2018). An excellent example of mixed migration is the Honduran Caravan marching across Mexico on its way to the US and migrants arriving in Europe and North America every year from Africa and Asia. Between 2015 and 2017, 68 percent of the 1.5 million refugees and economic migrants arriving in Europe landed in Greece, another 29 percent arrived in Italy, while the remaining three percent arrived in Spain. Most of these refugees and migrants were from Syria, Afghanistan, and Iraq (Borton and Collinson 2017). In 2016, Panamanian authorities registered 22,000 "extra-regional" migrants across the border from Colombia into Panama heading to the US (Dixon et al. 2018), which is the new single first-world destination as I shall argue in chapter 4.

CONCLUSION

To sum up briefly, the so-called global governance of migration is a political language that obscures the necropolitical objectives of a managerial approach to migration. It constructs migration as a phenomenon that is either voluntary or involuntary. Involuntary migration has been grounded on the refugee's legal category, which describes people who have a well-founded fear of persecution because of their political opinions, ethnicity, nationality, religion, and belonging to a specific social group. Those who claim protection under refugee international law, in a given country other than their own, are asylum seekers.

According to the asylum and refugee regime, a refugee is a person who has a well-founded fear of persecution because of their political opinions, ethnicity, nationality, religion, and belonging to a social group with specific characteristics. Africa, the Americas, and Europe have included indiscriminate violence and threats to life and security either as legitimate causes of persecution or as the basis for granting subsidiary and human rights protection. The merging of the refugee and human rights regimes have management purposes. The refugee definition served the political objectives of specific international wars and conflicts, such as the First and Second World Wars, and even Decolonization and the Cold War. Today the category has become insufficient to grasp the policy and legal needs of contemporary involuntary migration produced by forced depopulation. Apart from the refugee, involuntary migration also includes internally displaced persons, people in refugee-like situations, and people receiving subsidiary protection.

The forced migrant is a category with no rights attached and no binding obligation for the international community. While states have legally binding obligations when becoming a party to international and regional instruments of the regime, they are not obligated to grant refugee status to every individual claiming asylum; sovereignty allows them to establish the national institutions and criteria for processing asylum claims individually and for making decisions. Recent legal approaches, especially the Global Compact for Safe, Orderly, and Regular Migration and the Global Compact on Refugees, are non-binding instruments intended to prevent asylum seekers and undocumented migrants from reaching the West while transferring the responsibility for refugee crises to third world countries and ensuring benefits for international business.

NOTE

1. I have discussed in depth the problems with human rights discourses' truth affects in necropolitics, especially for women and asylum seekers in the US and Canada. More specifically, I have argued elsewhere that the public-private divide invisibilizes the nature of contemporary political power in which criminals work for the state and the military and the police have links with organized crime. As for women, I contend that human rights discourses' private/public divide obscures the importance of hegemonic masculinities in a human rights ontology that indeed assumes the particularities of violence affecting women. See: Estévez, Ariadna. 2013. "The Politics Of Death In Mexico: Dislocating Human Rights And Asylum Law Through Hybrid Agents." *Glocalism: Journal of Culture, Politics and Innovation* (1): 1–28. Estévez, Ariadna. 2017. "La gubernamentalización necropolítica del Estado y la masculinidad hegemónica: dislocación y recomposición ontológica de los derechos humanos," *Derecho y Crítica Social*, vol. 3, no. 1: 45–74.

Chapter 4

Managing Forced Migration

Once forced depopulation and lucrative death-produced migration, there are only criminal means of reaching the first world if neighboring third-world countries are not an option. People who become forced migrants with the forceful hope (Elliot 2016) of finding a new life used to go to countries with relatives and friends or colonial cultural ties such as language. Europe and North America have been the preferred destinations, although Australia, New Zealand, and Japan have become popular among displaced people from Asia and the Pacific islands. However, Europe has progressively shut down its continental borders, forcing migrants to opt for routes and destinations defined by availability instead of proximity or cultural ties. Transatlantic routes are available due to a transnational network of corruption and clandestine channels of distribution of illegal commodities, that is, cocaine and a global web of smugglers and organized crime groups. As North America (the US and Canada) has become the last rich destination left, Central America has become a "global pathway" to the US (United Nations Office on Drugs and Crime 2012). Forced migrants from all over the world—Africa, Asia, South America, and the Caribbean—travel through a necropolitical bottleneck plagued with crime and natural dangers, where thousands die, and only a few survive to carry on with their journey.

While chapter 2 examined the production of forced migration, the structural functioning of the apparatus, chapter 3 gave an overview of how the international asylum and refugee regime became part of the global governmentality of migration that uses human rights discourses and categories to apply the rule of law nercropower's legal principle of *pro morituri*. The argument in chapter 4 is that once it produces the conditions for forced migration to exist, the rule of law necropowers conduce migrants across deathly geographies where a web of necropolitical governmentalized states allow for criminal gangs to smuggle, traffic, extort, and ultimately kill forced migrants. Those who do not end up dead have to face the rule of law necropowers' enforcement of asylum and migration laws under the necropolitical legal principle of *pro morituri*. Therefore, the necropolitical apparatus of forced migration deploys a strategy of management based on a narrow, *pro morituri* understanding of the refugee. It contains three strategies: the *transnational necropolitical nomosphere*, the enforcement of *pro morituri asylum laws*, and dumping deported and refugee-to-be migrants in border cities' *pockets of disposability*.

Therefore, the chapter will first argue that a *transnational necropolitical nomosphere* allows for a global gateway to North America through Central America and Mexico. African, Asian, and Central American migrants become the disposable subject of the apparatus necropolitical production and management of forced migration. It will go on to discuss *pro morituri asylum laws* and the concept of *pockets of disposability*.

THE TRANSNATIONAL NECROPOLITICAL NOMOSPHERE

The spatial shift in the social sciences and the law owes much to geographers Henri Lefevbre and David Harvey, who argued for the social construction of space to understand how the cities are ordered and organized along the lines of class and the reproduction of capital. Social space is a social and historical construction (Delgado Mahecha 2003: 80), but Harvey explicitly refers to time as a critical variable. Harvey's interpretation of time *vis a vis* space has been vital in interpretations of globalization, which he defined as an experience of compression of the time-space relationship (Harvey 2006: 135–146). Geographer Doreen Massey questioned and broadened these authors' work, saying that there are race and gender differences in the way individuals experience time/space compressions in global capitalism. Although Massey is a structuralist just as Lefebvre and Harvey, she dismisses class determinism to argue that recognition of gender and race in the study of space goes beyond ethics; it is conceptual accuracy defining a "global sense of place," that is, a sense of how subjectivity defines the perception of time-space compression (Massey 2008: 262). Subjects experience time and space according to their experiences as racialized and gendered bodies.

Edward W. Soja (2009) has a similar view, but his work relates to the law's spatialization. Soja's idea of spatial (in)justice contends that wealth and poverty are geographically distributed along the lines of class, race, and gender (Soja 2009). Soja believes that "the political organization of space . . . is a particularly powerful source of spatial injustice." He also claims that: "Geographically uneven development and underdevelopment provides another framework for interpreting the processes that produce injustices, but as with other processes, it is only when this unevenness rigidifies into more lasting structures of privilege and advantage that intervention becomes necessary" (Soja 2009: 3). Necropolitical governmentalized states enforce spatial injustice through the apparatus of necropolitical production and management of forced migration. The enforcement of law and policy organizes space to manage international forced migration, producing death along with race, gender, and class lines. Dehm claims that:

> the actions of state decision-makers, for example, have not only forced migrants to undertake more dangerous and deadly journeys to avoid ever-proliferating state practices of unauthorized migrant detection, interception, and deportation, but such state actions have also sought to leverage the physical environment as part of state regimes of border control premised on the logic of deterrence. This emergent mode of border control has been termed "governing through death" to refer to state strategies of consciously allowing people travelling without state authorization to be abandoned to the physical forces of deserts and seas (Dhem 2020: 9).

Chapter 1 discussed David Delaney's concept of the nomosphere to argue that necropower's dystopic law enforcement created permanent irregular settings or scenarios to facilitate lucrative death. According to Delaney, a nomosphere is the spatialization of law according to specific ideologies and objectives (Delaney 2010). While nomospheres are spatialized according to state borders and work differently in the first and third worlds, the spatialization of law in the apparatus of forced migration is transnational. It operates according to what Hardt and Negri (2000) called *network power*: a chain of organizations and governments aimed at regulating and controlling goods and people according to racialized economic interest. The transnational necropolitical nomosphere is the space organized for the lucrative regulation of death through a network of permanently irregular, corrupted, and death-productive legal systems. It is a web of necropolitical national nomospheres instrumentalizing impunity, crime, and environmental conditions for migrants' lucrative death.

THE GEOGRAPHY OF THE TRANSNATIONAL NECROPOLITICAL NOMOSPHERE

While third-world countries receive the bulk of regional refugees—Colombia receives Venezuelans; South Africa, Zimbabweans; India, Bangladeshis—rich nations are preferred destinations for thousands of international forced migrants. However, rich countries have radically shut down their borders to forced migrants, including people fleeing from criminal violence, environmental degradation, and political conflict. In recent years, Europe stopped receiving asylum claims in its embassies and imposed penalties on commercial transport. Recent EU legislation establishes that people seeking asylum must apply in the first European nation they arrive in, without the opportunity of choosing a destination according to family networks or colonial and cultural ties. Greece and Italy—and their archipelagos—are the countries bordering Asia and African, so they receive and return the bulk of claims.

However, what has shut down the so-called Balkan route to Europe, is the 2016 European Union-Turkey Agreement. The facto closing of European borders has left North America as the only rich destination for people from Asia, Africa, South America, the Caribbean, and Central America. Global forced migrants head towards the US through dangerous and long land and sea routes: "Instead of heading North Europe, where the crisis at sea has led to thousands of deaths in the Mediterranean, a number of migrants . . . are now choosing to fly across the Atlantic on a route that goes first to Latin America and then north through Mexico to the United States and Canada" (Dixon et al. 2018).

Transatlantic routes become available due to a transnational necropolitical nomosphere in which corruption networks, clandestine distribution channels for illegal products such as cocaine, and a global network of migrant smugglers make trafficking and smuggling a millionaire criminal business. Both routes, Europe and North America, are the most profitable business for smugglers. They smuggle 55,000 people annually from Africa to Europe in a 150-million-dollar business, and 3 million from South and Central America and the Caribbean to North America, in a 6.6 billion worth market (United Nations Office on Drugs and Crime 2010: 59, 67). In general, smuggling is a 6.75-billion-a-year business (Dixon et al. 2018).

Migrant smugglers operating in Bangladesh, Ecuador, and Colombia are working together with well-established networks of government officials and commercial airlines, facilitating cocaine smuggling from Colombia to Europe via Eastern Europe (Bosnia) and Africa (Guinea Bissau, Niger, Zimbabwe, and South Africa). Colombian guerrilla groups and criminal organizations (FARC, Rastrojos, Clan del Golfo), and Mexican drug cartels (Sinaloa, Jalisco Nueva Generación), outsource smuggling services to local and traditional networks in Ecuador. They make huge profits out of people smuggling and sex trafficking (Cohen 2019). Álvarez Velasco claims that "Ecuador has come to be a zone of transit for international migrants. For at least the past eight years, people from Asia, Africa, the Caribbean, and the Middle East have increasingly arrived in the country intending to move to other destinations, mainly to the US in the North and Brazil, Chile, and Argentina to the south" (Álvarez Velasco 2016: par. 8).

Criminal networks charge between 10,000 and 20,000 dollars for getting people from Africa and Asia to Brazil, Colombia, or Ecuador. Cohen (2019) claims that Brazil became a key spot for the transatlantic drug trade due to corruption and a weak law enforcement culture. Illegal groups from Nigeria and Serbia use Sao Paulo as their business headquarters for cocaine trafficking to Europe through South Africa, Zimbabwe, and Guinea Bissau. Mexican and Colombian criminal organizations have headquarters in Guinea Bissau. Also, commercial flights use to go to Mali through Venezuela, facilitating cocaine trafficking. Since 2015, criminals use this illegal transatlantic infrastructure to bring people from Africa and Asia. Given yesteryear's mafia ties between Senegal, Nigeria, Niger, and Guinea Bissau with Brazil, large numbers of trafficking and human trafficking, both labor and sexual, start in Brazil. As InsightCrime argues: "This highly organized smuggling ring operated across two continents, maintained smuggling contacts in at least eight countries and created credible false documents that permitted the migrants to seek asylum and board commercial flights" (Chaparro 2019: par. 9).

When arriving in Brazil, Africans and Asians who do not reach Ecuador directly get to Ecuador from there since it has the most open visa policy in the world. When the Ecuador-Spain migration intensified with increasing racism and closing doors in Europe, in 2008, Ecuador made a constitutional reform that established its open-door policy for everyone, with an automatic tourist visa for ninety days. Human trafficking from Asia and Africa to Ecuador erased that six months later: Ecuador imposed visas on various Asian nationalities (China, Afghanistan, Bangladesh, Pakistan, Eritrea, Ethiopia, Kenya, Nepal, Nigeria, and Somalia) (Freier and Freier 2013). Nevertheless, this continues to be a port of entry from Asia, Africa, Cuba, and Venezuela because of the extensive network of corruption and independent smugglers and the falsification of passports that allow migrants to move freely through Central America and the Southern Cone. Towards the Southern Cone, human trafficking also becomes sexual trafficking in countries like Colombia. With an Ecuadorian passport, migrants can have a safe-conduct throughout the continent (Bonello 2019, Chaparro 2019, United Nations Office on Drugs and Crime 2012, Dixon et al. 2018).

While Colombian authorities blame Europe for the increasing number of transatlantic migrants arriving in Colombia, these are not the only migrants arriving in Colombia or Brazil on their way to the US. Asylum seekers from Venezuela, the Dominican Republic, Haiti, and Cuba arrive there to start their journey, by land, to the US and Canada, through Central America. Local smugglers take over and charge between 10,000 and 20,000 to get people to the US via the Darien Gap. According to scholar Soledad Alvarez, organized crime has incorporated independent smuggling into broader transnational criminal networks. Smugglers carry different goods like arms and drugs, so humans are just another commodity to trade with (Bonello 2019, Chaparro 2019, United Nations Office on Drugs and Crime 2012, Dixon et al. 2018).

In the Central American route, many Endriago subjects (Valencia 2010) smuggle, kidnap, traffic, and kill migrants across dangerous geographies that become the only possible way because of border controls. The Darien Gap, a sixty-mile rainforest separating Colombia from Panama, is a naturally dangerous zone because it is a deep tropical land full of poisonous fauna and flora, sinuous and mighty rivers, and stiff and slippery cliffs to cross for most people. Its natural density also made it conducive to criminal and guerrilla activities in yesteryear; today, such groups as the Colombian FARC and drug cartels such as Clan del Golfo use their knowledge of the forest to extort migrants crossing the Darien Gap (Polo Alvis, Enrique, and Manrique Lara 2018, Matta and Herrera 2019). Panamanian authorities claim that in 2016 alone, some 22,000 global migrants crossed the Colombia-Panama border. Mexico detained 2,958 African migrants in 2018 (Bonello 2019). Once they make it to Panama, they get another smuggler to cross Mexico, which has become very securitized since 2018. Some migrants ask for asylum or regularization in order to avoid being the target of organized crime. However, many do not want to stay in Mexico.

For migrants, Mexico is what Eduardo González Velázquez (2011) called "the vertical border." He points out that the violent conditions that migrants find in the Guatemala-Mexico border travel with them all along their journey throughout Mexico towards the northern border. Mexico is all a "border zone," a 3,500 km vertical border with natural and geographical hazards and extreme weather. The vertical border is also plagued with criminals and other subjects that see migrants as "disposable commodities" (Treviño 2020), subjects of lucrative death. Criminals, gangs, migration officials, police officers, the military, smugglers, and sex and labor traffickers are all Endriagos (Valencia 2010) that rob, kidnap, extort, slave or use them for money or the illegal trade of sex and organs (González Velázquez 2011). Drug cartels force them to become *sicarios* and drug dealers, and in the case of women, sex slaves. As discussed in chapter 1, all kinds of Endriagos cannibalize migrants to their exhaustion.

People who survive the vertical border find further obstacles—this time through *pro morituri* asylum laws in the US and pockets of disposability in the US-Mexico border.

PRO MORITURI ASYLUM LAWS

The US has always regulated the "whiteness" of its population through migration policy and law. The anti-Chinese and anti-Irish laws, and Mexican guest worker programs, have allowed the US to regulate race and culture as a form of immunization (Esposito 2005) against widespread migration.[1] For Americans, people fleeing violence are no different from undocumented "economic" migrants, the pathogen immunized (Esposito 2005) through progressive policy and law. Security controls regulate migration through asylum but not the same way they used to do—a political tool for states to punish their enemies. Now the US enforces asylum and refugee laws with the necropolitical legal principle of *pro morituri*, making and interpreting law through the less favorable legal standard for asylum seekers.

The American asylum discourse includes several legal categories that construct the subject suffering from persecution. Asylum law defines the refugee in terms of the United Nations Convention Relating to the Status of Refugees (1951) and its Protocol (1967). The law also includes withholding of removal, which implements the obligation of nonrefoulment established in the Convention of Refugees; and the prevention of deportation due to a well-founded fear of being the subject of torture, enforced as a complementary means of protection under the Convention against Torture (CAT) and Other Cruel, Inhuman or Degrading Treatment or Punishment.

I argued elsewhere (Estévez 2017) that the American regime was biopolitics of population management. This biopolitics works through a sizable institutional framework that includes courts, immigration offices, and law firms. As biopolitics, asylum works as a means to exclude most displaced people because the majority failed to fulfill the restricted criteria of the mainstream definition of the refugee—see chapter 3. However, more recently, asylum and refugee laws and policies exclude the majority while also leaving thousands to die –the rule of law necropower's enforcement of *pro morituri* asylum laws.

As part of US migration governmentality, the government enforces asylum law managerially, although its reproduction, signification, and power techniques resemble sovereign power, such as the courts. In the words of Gibney, "The United States essentially has had no refugee policy as such—only an immigration policy disguised as a refugee policy" (Gibney 2000: 53). A twofold managerial apparatus deploys the neoliberal governmentality of migration: the biopolitics of a semijudicial asylum system; and the *pro morituri* principle when interpreting asylum laws and making policy.

The Biopolitics of the American Asylum Regime

As biopolitics, the asylum system excludes a subject a priori if they have: participated in the persecution of others in connection with one or more of the five protected grounds; stayed in the US for over a year at the time of the application; or resettled successfully in another country. Once a person is eligible for asylum, their claim will be successful if they manage to prove, according to the Immigration and Nationality Act (INA) and customary law, that they have a well-founded fear of persecution due to the government's unwillingness or inability to protect them from their persecutors. Also, they have to show that this persecution is motivated by the victim's race, nationality, religion, political opinion, or membership of a particular social group. These two concepts—the government's unwillingness or inability to protect and motivation—determine the scope of the construction of the subject of asylum law.

As stated previously, in biopolitics, the law is used to homogenize populations. In this case, there are openly managerial features in the enforcement of asylum law that show how instruments intended for the administration of international justice—such as the Refugee Covenant included in the INA—are used to regulate immigration to the US. American migration courts are administrative, managerial bodies that administrate migration rather than disciplinary bodies controlling sovereign power. The quasi-legal or quasi-administrative character of migration courts makes decision-making subjective and arbitrary. Immigration courts in the US are not constitutional like civil or criminal courts where people can claim rights. According to Cabot (Interview, 2012), immigration courts are "court-like (although) it's actually an administrative body." Claimants appeal courts' decisions at the Board of Immigration Appeals, whose published decisions are law only for the circuit where the claim was based. Only when the asylum seeker appeals a judge's decision in the Supreme Court does their case enter a constitutional field. Although these administrative bodies look like courts, law enforcement is relaxed and discretionary.

Cabot argues that the law "can be changed based on the judge who oversees the court . . . each particular judge can alter the rules within their own court and so this gives the judges much more discretionary powers than judges in other courts in the US, criminal courts, civil courts . . . to change the rules to suit their own biases and preconceptions that they do in another arenas." Since "immigration judge decisions are not law, they're not precedential published decisions, so one immigration judge that starts to give asylum to people from Mexico fleeing violence doesn't mean that by law the whole border is now open, it's still a decision-by-decision thing" (Cabot, Interview, 2012).

The arbitrariness of asylum discourse is also dependent on the division of asylum into affirmative and defensive procedures. This division permits differential treatment of claimants according to their socioeconomic status and gender, which supposedly determines their criminal proclivity. Affirmative applicants enter the country with a valid visa or those who overstay their visas and therefore hold no documents authorizing them to remain in the country. An asylum officer from the US Office of Immigration and Citizenship

Services (USCIS) reviews these claims. If they decide not to approve a claim, they refer it to an immigration judge of the Executive Office for Immigration Review (EOIR), a US Department of Justice branch but fails to operate as a proper court. Only then is the applicant transferred to removal proceedings, although their application has not yet been rejected. The denial letter explains: "This is not a denial of your asylum application. You may request asylum again before the immigration judge, and your request will be considered (without additional refiling) when you appear before an immigration judge on the date and at the time listed on the attached charging document."

Many asylum seekers who pass through a court are in the defensive asylum, although they began affirmative procedures. Immigration officers who deny asylum in affirmative proceedings do not give in-depth legal arguments when informing them of their decisions. They only state that the applicants have failed to prove past or future persecution but do not explain why. In defensive claims, a migration officer places the applicant in removal proceedings, and the case goes directly to the EOIR. Typically, claimants who opt directly for defensive asylum do not own a visa and state their intention to seek asylum at a port of entry before an immigration officer. In these situations, asylum seekers are sent to detention centers where they remain until an immigration court decides, which could take up to five years. While awaiting the judge's decision,[2] applicants can request a "credible fear" interview, that is, an interview in which asylum seekers have to provide evidence that their fear of persecution is well-founded. The judge then either grants or denies asylum and proceeds to removal (Roitman Rosenmann 2005). The success of the claimant's credible fear interview depends entirely on the judge's perception. In terms of the asylum procedure, credible fear is not the same as "reasonable fear," which is the basis for the suspension of the removal proceedings for people who are not eligible for asylum but still face death or torture, according to the Refugee Convention and the Convention Against Torture.

Crystal Massey, a human rights advocate and researcher at the Southwest Asylum and Migration Institute—which deals with Mexican cases in El Paso, Texas, and Las Cruces, New Mexico—claims that the affirmative/defensive divide has no other objective than to serve as a filter for the type of Mexicans who can access the asylum system. Passing the first filter does not mean they were granted asylum, just access to the system. Massey argues that people who hold a visa are usually middle-class, well-informed Mexicans who have the means or the knowledge to obtain a border crossing document or know that stating an interest in asylum at the border will place them in detention. These are not economic migrants. Massey also claims that young men spend more time in detention; these are the men associated with the drug business or gangs in the biased mind of American civil servants or judges. In detention, people are ill-treated (forced to remain in degrading and uncomfortable conditions for extended periods) or harassed (separated from young children and told they could remain separated for a very long time) to pressure them to drop their asylum claim.

Pro Morituri Legal Interpretation of Asylum Laws

Although the semijudicial character of the apparatus is key to defining the managerial status of asylum law in general, legal texts play a fundamental role in the regulation of global migration. Although it lacks normative content, asylum law has truth effects concerning what constitutes an act, and a victim of persecution and the context in which persecution occurs—the use of human rights law further reinforces these truth effects (see chapter 3). It creates a politics of truth—the establishment of subjectivities, objects, and concepts that separate true from false—in which the definitions of state attribution, responsibility, context, and victim exclude many subjectivities, objects, and concepts.

The case of asylum seekers fleeing *lucrative death* and *forced depopulation* (chapter 3) falls outside this politics of truth since *sicarios* usually work for the police or the army, or the army and the police work for the cartels. The politics of truth of asylum discourse-reinforced with human rights treaties such as the CAT—and the particularity of the production of forced migration are the basis for a narrow interpretation of two legal categories: (1) a well-founded fear of present or future persecution due to the state's unwillingness or inability to protect them; and (2) that they are or could be the victims of persecution due to their nationality, race, religion, political opinion, or membership of a particular social group.

Firstly, courts interpret fear of persecution as fear of severe harm and the state's failure to provide protection *vis a vis* this possibility. Judges interpret persecution in its political view as discussed in chapter 3, more specifically as sustained and systematic human rights abuses indicating the state's failure to protect and in which the level of harm must be severe (Price 2006).

By interpreting fear of persecution in its limited political view, judges apply the *pro morituri* principle because most cases of people fleeing forced depopulation and lucrative death do not fill the criteria—especially if persecutors are corporations or criminals—and are unable to provide proof. Judges could widen their interpretation of persecution and social group, but they prefer the narrowest reading. In order to demonstrate persecution, a person's experience must be more than simple unpleasantness, harassment, or even essential suffering. According to the *UN Asylum Handbook*, persecution could be an action of the state or result from the state's inability to control the criminality of non-state actors (García 2011, Pickering 2005). There are two interpretations of persecution by non-state agents in the face of which the state is willing but unable to provide protection. One, the view of protection, in which the definition is extended to cover situations where the state of origin is incapable of providing the necessary protection; and two, the view of accountability, which establishes that only when persecution is by the state can the person be considered a refugee (Bruin 2002).

Mexican and Central American cases are marked by the systematic participation of alleged private actors. This is not the problem per se, as Cabot explains: "that issue, in my opinion at least, is not the most pressing issue because in some ways in asylum law this unwilling or unable clause . . . it doesn't even matter for asylum law whether the police are involved or not, to some extent because whether they're involved, maybe they're unwilling to stop the violence, if they're not, maybe they're unable to stop the violence." The non-state actor issue is problematic for protection provided under the CAT since protection is only for people who have been tortured or could be tortured by state officials or with the acquiescence of the state. If a claimant cannot prove persecution based on one of the five protected grounds, this possible avenue of protection is also closed if there is no state involvement. According to Cabot and Oretskin, for Mexican claimants, the main issue is to prove the inability or unwillingness of the Mexican government to protect its citizens from persecution or torture by state authorities or criminals. As Oretskin puts it, in the end, "the key always is, no matter whether political opinion or social group, the government or representative of the government is incapable or unwilling to protect you." In the opinion of Oretskin, it is necessary to have a tie to the government, so the tying of cartels to the government is the missing piece in legal strategies.

In terms of asylum law, the difficulty of proving governments' complicity with drug cartels, gangs, and corporations is related to such factors as law enforcement officials being on the payroll of cartels, even though the state enforces antidrug programs, sometimes at a binational level with the US itself. In order to prove the state's inability or unwillingness to fight drug cartels, the lawyers of claimants submit to the USCIS or EOIR recommendations from Mexican human rights commissions or news clippings reporting that law enforcement officials or soldiers directly participated in, or ignored, murders related to the case. However, these are not always forthcoming, and testimonies may be the only available proof. In response, asylum authorities use evidence of Mexican or bilateral policy in the fight against drug trafficking. Secondly, given the characteristics of the Mexican situation, arguing motivation is never straightforward either. As Cabot claims: "when you're dealing with people who are fleeing from drug violence, there's no obvious group, no obvious ground . . . you know, it's not their race, religion, nationality, so those go out the window." Therefore, asylum claimants have only two category options: political opinion and membership of a particular social group. However, given the characteristics of the war on drugs, the connections to political opinions or social groups are evident only in the most traditional cases.

Political opinion refers to "any opinion on any matter in which the machinery of the State, government, and policy may be engaged" (Buchanan 2010: 46). Even if the applicant has not yet expressed their opinions, the strength of their convictions leads to the assumption that the applicant will eventually express them and enter into conflict with authorities (Buchanan 2010). To date, people who have managed to demonstrate a well-founded fear of persecution due to their political opinions are those expressing a political opinion in terms of the INA and the UN Convention, that is, typical asylum seekers. In the words of Cabot (Interview, 2012): "For some people fleeing Mexico there's political opinion, that actually works for them, but that's usually politicians, journalists or human rights activists, so that's specifically for people who speak out, and doesn't apply just to the normal person fleeing violence."

As for membership of a particular social group, in most cases, the reasons cited by applicants are not explicitly those of the INA and the UN Convention—that is, persecution by sicarios and corrupt law enforcement officials of entire families who either refuse to pay extortion or speak out about extortion; or the killing of relatives of people murdered when seeking justice. More specifically, in some legal circuits, a particular social group must have the following three key characteristics: social visibility, immutability, and particularity. Visibility means the applicant must be a well-known member of the group they claim to belong to and show proof of this—that is, appear in media coverage of a demonstration if they are an activist or have signed articles if they are a journalist. People refusing to pay quotas to cartels or seeking justice for a relative who was disappeared by force is extremely difficult since people do not want to be visible.

Immutability refers to people who share innate or unalterable characteristics such as their past, defined by something as necessary as their identity that they should not be required to abandon (Buchanan 2010, Pickering 2005). Also, there is no voluntary relationship or innate characteristic to bind its members (García 2011). For example, police officers (law enforcement officers in general) could be granted asylum on account of their membership of a particular group because they have a "shared past experience" and share "a common immutable characteristic," which is having been law enforcement officials, a feature that cannot be changed (Buchanan 2010, Pickering 2005). Therefore, people who refuse to pay quotas to drug cartels, criminal informants, Mexicans returning from the US, and businesspersons (wealthy merchants or families) form categories that are too broad to qualify as a particular group.

To sum up, the biopolitical management of forced migration is possible due to the asylum system's bureaucratic rather than judicial features. Asylum law is applied to normalize and manage applicants, not to provide international protection for people with a well-founded fear of persecution. The law intends to create the necessary legal texts to justify the refusal of appeals from future asylum seekers. Asylum law, which usually corresponds to sovereign power, therefore, comes to play a biopolitical role. As shown here, this is made possible by an asylum apparatus supported by the semijudicial asylum system and the ambiguity of asylum law. Firstly, the "court-like" nature of the system permits judges to be subjective in their decision-making. The affirmative/defensive divide in the asylum procedure serves as a filter through which only middle-class claimants can avoid detention. Secondly, the well-founded fear of persecution, the unwillingness or inability of the government to protect victims from their persecutors, and persecution for reasons of political opinion or membership of a particular social group are all used as biopolitical tactics. Judges interpret the law through the necropolitical *pro morituri* principle and choose not to expand the legal concept of asylum and prefer to narrow their interpretations as a means of denying this option to people fleeing violence.

Pro Morituri Asylum Law-Making

The US's asylum system was already tough on people fleeing forced depopulation and lucrative death, but President Donald Trump is applying the *pro morituri* principle to law-making and interpretation. Waslin (2020) claims that since he took office in late 2016, Trump carries out an "unorthodox" use of presidential legal privileges. She argues that American presidents have issued executive orders and proclamations with political purposes in a historical perspective, but Trump has issued them to deliver immigration policy *de facto* and dismiss Congress while doing it (Waslin 2020).

According to Waslin's quantitative analysis of executive orders and proclamations since 1945, Trump has issued 10 out of the 56 immigration-related executive orders and 9 out of the 64 proclamations. Also, 8 percent of Trump's executive orders have been immigration-related. He issued these proclamations and executive orders for policy direction, a reinterpretation of current laws, or instruct law enforcement agencies. He has produced up to 20 percent of these political tools to make the country's migration policy without consulting the Legislative Power, preventing the opposition from disagreeing with his *pro morituri* law-making. The American Congress is highly diverse. Up to 22 percent of the House of Representatives and Senate belong to ethnic minorities. Minorities include blacks, native Americans, Asians, and of course, Latinos (Pew Research Center 2019). It is unclear whether Trump's unique use of executive powers responds to his authoritarian personality or his openly racist views of migration. He “often exercises his executive authority without much process, circumventing the well-established procedures for consultation and securing input from Congress, federal agencies, White House staff, and the public” (Waslin 2020: 64). He issued most of his immigration-related executive orders when the Republican Party held the Congress’ majority. However, he uses his executive power to halt migration and asylum claims asserting his openly racist view of migration from Mexico and Central America.

In early 2017, he issued three executive orders enhancing border control, increasing deportations, and limiting asylum and refugee status (Center for Migration Studies 2020). The first order was the Border Security and Immigration Enforcement Improvements, which infamously focused on building a 2,000-mile border wall, increasing the construction of (private) detention centers, hiring other 5,000 Border Patrol agents, and expanding expedited deportations (The White House 2017a). As for asylum, the second order, the Enhancing Public Safety in the Interior of the United States, targeted deportation. Therefore, it banned sanctuary cities and encouraged prison authorities to cooperate with the Department of Homeland Security’s Immigration and Customs Enforcement (ICE) to identify undocumented migrants in jail so they can deport them. Immigrants who have committed a criminal offense could be deported—including such offenses as working without a permit. In order to carry out this, the order established the hire of 10,000 new ICE agents (The White House 2017b).

Finally, the Protecting the Nation from Terrorist Attacks by Foreign Nationals suspended visas for up to 90 days to citizens of countries found harmful to the US’ interests (Iran, Iraq, Sudan, Syria, Libya, Somalia, and Yemen) and ceased the resettlement of Syrian nationals indefinitely. It also shut down its refugee program for 120 days, which prevented any person seeking asylum from applying for refugee status in American territory during that period. It also reduced the refugee quota from 110,000 to (Penn State Law 2020) 50,000 a year (*The New York Times* 2017). Later that year, Trump reinforced the anti-Muslim policy banning the entrance of citizens from Chad, Libya, North Korea, and Somalia, and severely limited temporary work visas and green cards, and a progressive dismantling of the Deferred Action for Childhood Arrivals (DACA).[3] Finally, Trump ordered to end the Temporary Protection Status for Haiti, Nicaragua, and El Salvador.

By April 2018, more *pro morituri* policy and law worsened the situation for asylum seekers. The Attorney General issued the Zero Tolerance policy, which made undocumented immigration a criminal offense—it used to be an administrative offense only. The Attorney General’s Office’s justification was that undocumented immigration had increased by 203 percent between

March 2017 and March 2018 (The United States Department of Justice 2018). Therefore, the Border Patrol arrested migrants and took them to prison. However, the law forbids keeping children in criminal detention, so authorities sent migrants' children to immigration detention centers. It was a scandal. Even Trump's allies criticized this measure for inhumane and its instrumentalization for children's sexual and human trafficking.

Nevertheless, while only 46 percent of immigrants arrested by Border Patrol agents were prosecuted, preferring those adults carrying children. Over 3,000 children were separated from their parents, which means that "Family separation was therefore not an unintended consequence of the 'zero-tolerance' policy but an effort to punish families," according to a Human Rights Watch's brief (Human Rights Watch 2018). This policy radicalized San Diego's Operation Streamline, which was first enforced in early 2018 and increased prosecutions of undocumented migrants by 1200 percent, targeting parents as a means to force families from immigrating (ACLU San Diego 2018). By June that year, Trump issued Executive Order Affording Congress an Opportunity to Address Family Separation, which put an end to family separation (The White House 2018).

In October 2018, an estimated 3,500-migrant caravan from Honduras marched through Mexico towards the US. The group included whole families, single women with their children, gay and transexual men fleeing homophobia, women escaping sex violence, and trying to save their male children from forced enrollment in gangs. President Trump threatened further militarizing the US-Mexico border if the Honduran migrants reached the frontier. Rancher militias also prepared their guns to receive the caravan. Trump responded by announcing in December the Migrant Protection Protocols (MPP), referred to as "Remain in Mexico Policy," which established that "certain" aliens arriving at American entry points without papers would have to wait in Mexico for their asylum procedures to be resolved. The protocols were enforced in January 2019, mainly targeting immigrants from Honduras and Central America in general (Department of Homeland Security 2019c).

By July 2018, the Department of Homeland Security and the Department of Justice adopted an Interim Final Rule, which established that asylum seekers who failed to apply for and be denied asylum in a safe third country were "ineligible for asylum" in the United States (Department of Homeland Security 2019a). For Trump, safe third countries were Mexico and Central America. In early September, the US Supreme Court endorsed Trump's Remain in Mexico Policy, saying that it was legal that asylum seekers were forced to apply for asylum and remain in a Safe Third Country while awaiting, even though these measures openly violate the rights on Non-Refoulment and to Due Process. In February 2020, the 9th US Circuit Court of Appeals blocked the policy but held its decision as Trump argued that lifting the policy in the Southwestern border would encourage migrants to "rush to the border." In March 2020, amid the COVID□19 lockdown, the Supreme Court said the policy could stay in effect while the policy's legal challenges were resolved (Álvarez 2020a, De Vogue 2020). By January 2020, Trump had signed Safe Third Country agreements—called Asylum Cooperative Agreements—with El Salvador, Honduras, and Guatemala. A Homeland Security interim final rule issued in November 2019 allowed Trump to enforce the agreements, starting with the Guatemala agreement (Department of Homeland Security 2019b, Narea 2019).

Trump's *pro morituri* law-making and interpretation is a necropolitical strategy to transfer its territorial borders to the third world, leading people to deathly spaces and situations. A couple of months after MPPs were first enforced, August 2019—the asylum waiting list in Tijuana (which existed for years) had stretched to over 10,000. Only 34 people a day were allowed to cross (a Border Patrol-controlled system known as the Metering), and the waiting time was 6–9 months. By early 2019, only Tijuana, Nogales, Ciudad Juárez, Piedras Negras, and Nuevo Laredo had over 100 people waiting lists (a total of 4,900 people). By August, Mexicali, San Luis Colorado, Agua Prieta, Ciudad Acuña, Reynosa, and Matamoros had waiting lists. Altogether, these cities are processing over 26,000 names in asylum waiting lists, and courts have returned 32,000 people in asylum proceedings. A total of 58,000 asylum seekers got stranded along the Mexican border in 16 cities. Tijuana has the largest waiting least, while Ciudad Juárez has more returned people (13,100) (Kao and Lu 2019). Shelters in other cities—Matamoros, Nuevo Laredo—were overcrowded and unable to take more migrants, pushing them to sleep in the streets. Some 6,400 returned to their countries, helped by the Mexican government (Kao and Lu 2019).

In September 2019, tent courts opened in Nuevo Laredo and Brownsville, Texas, to process the bulk of asylum claims produced under MPP (Álvarez 2019). The government did not open the tent courts to journalists until January 2020, who reported that asylum claimants do not get to face the judge; the hearings are on a teleconference, even before the COVID□19 lockdown. Because the tents are borderline, asylum seekers find it difficult to find counseling and legal advice for a legal-administrative that it was already difficult. Once the hearing finishes, people have to wait on the Mexican side until the next hearing, which could occur in months (Álvarez 2020b). Asylum seekers sleep rough next to the tents, which, according to *Forbes Magazine*, are run by the New York-based corporation Deployed Resources, responsible for the tents used in massive rock concerts such as Lollapalooza. The Department of Homeland Security paid Deployed Resources 48.9 million dollars to build the tents (Çam 2019). In February 2020, Trump also announced his intentions to increase appeals fees to almost 1,000. If the US was not making enough money out of its war against asylum, in February 2020, it announced an increase to the fees for immigration appeals. An immigration judge's ruling and the request for a case reconsideration or reopening before the Board of Immigration Appeals is 110 dollars, but if Trump's proposal succeeds, they would be 975 and 895 dollars, accordingly (Swales 2020).

According to a report by Refugees International, since the issue of the MPP, Trump had left some 60,000 asylum seekers stranded on Mexican territory awaiting hearings or resolutions of his asylum application, and another 15,000 are waiting to be able to apply. This fact, together with the fear provoked by COVID□19 and the murder of George Floyd by Minneapolis police officers in May 2020, encouraged asylum seekers, especially those coming from Africa and Haiti, to seek asylum in Mexico. However, following Ortega-Velázquez (2017), Mexico's Mexican asylum system is not much better than the US, even though asylum is a constitutional right—constitutional rights are for everyone, including foreigners.

In Mexico, the Refugees, Complementary Protection, and Political Asylum Law have fragmented the refugee category into political asylees, refugees, and people with complementary protection. People have 30 days to file a claim and are advised of the decision within up to 90 days. If denied asylum or refuge, they may appeal the decision within 15 days. However, the same asylum officers who rejected a claim in the first place are the same authorities reviewing appeals. Most of the time, their argument for denying asylum is, like in the US, the possibility of internal flight, which is not possible. Besides, migration officials do not inform migrants that they have the right to seek asylum when entering the country, and when people are aware of this right, authorities talk them out of it (Ortega-Vázquez 2017). Like in the US, in Mexico, asylum law and procedures are *pro morituri* since they are designed to prevent people from achieving refugee status.

In addition to legal barriers to the right to asylum, Mexico has lately become the US' guardian dog at its extraterritorial borders with Guatemala as part of its *pro morituri* law-making. The Mexican government had a moderate humanitarian policy toward Central American migrants when president Andrés Manuel López Obrador took office in late 2018. However, in June 2019, this tolerant attitude changed as Trump threatened his government to impose a 5 percent tariff on Mexican produce if the government failed to stop migration at the Mexico-Guatemala border within forty-five days with at least 6,000 members of the militarized national Guard. Mexico complied, sending 2,400 officers (Pradilla 2019a). In August, migrants from African and Haiti detained in the Siglo XXI detention center at Tapachula, Chiapas, started a series of protests against the Mexican government, demanding to continue their journey towards the US. Protesters claimed that migration officers asked them for 1500 dollars to get safe passage. In October 2019, the

National Guard and the Federal Police suppressed the protest and prevented them from continuing their trip to the North. By October, Africans continued their protests (Recamier 2019).

To sum up, the biopolitics of the asylum in the US becomes necropolitics when president Trump uses his rule of law necropower to legislate and enforce the law through the *pro morituri* principle.

DUMPING GLOBAL MIGRANTS IN DISPOSABILITY POCKETS

Chapter 3 argued that thousands of people flee criminal violence, development□led environmental devastation, and political repression crossing international borders in search of international protection in the US and Europe and transit countries such as Mexico. Likewise, as stated before in the chapter, global trafficking and smuggling networks bring people from Africa and Asia to Mexico's southern border and the US-Mexico border cities to reach the American Dream or even a safe haven in Mexico. In the meantime, President Trump's *pro morituri* laws have led to 32,000 returns (after the first hearing) and at least 9,300 pending asylum hearings from 2017 to mid-2019 (United Nations Office on Drugs and Crime 2012, Kao and Lu 2019)

While figures are terrifying, the absolute horror lies in the legal and life limbos these measures create. Ever-increasing returns, deportations, and asylum hearing waiting lists dispose of people in border cities such as Tijuana, in the northeastern state of Baja California, in Mexico. With no jobs, no money, and no certainty in their future, migrants find temporary shelter in Tijuana's riverbanks, under bridges, and even within the pipes of sewage systems. However, Tijuana is not the only place in Mexico where this is occurring. Other border cities along the Río Grande are becoming spaces where the US disposes asylum seekers (Kao and Lu 2019). Mexicali, San Luis Colorado, Nogales, Agua Prieta, Ciudad Juárez, Ciudad Acuña, Piedras Negras, Nuevo Laredo, Ciudad Miguel Alemán, Matamoros, and Reynosa. Most of these cities are in the Mexico Travel Advisory (Department of State 2020), therefore in addition to deprivation, asylum seekers are permanently exposed to crime (kidnapping, trafficking, forced labor for criminal groups, and murder) and illness because of the lack of sanitary measures and access to health and social services in general. These places are also occupied by homeless people (Aviña Cerecer 2020).

These spaces constitute a spatially contained legal and social limbo that leads to precarious conditions that, in turn, lead to death or illness. These open-air jails for asylum seekers and other displaced people I call *pockets of disposability*. In order to illustrate the construction of pockets of disposability through *pro morituri* asylum laws, the chapter will describe the situation of forced migrants deported to Tijuana, the Mexican border city neighboring San Diego.

Tijuana's Dumpsters

Due to its geographical location, Tijuana has become a shelter for all migrants—asylum seekers, irregular migrants, deportees—who become stranded. When arriving, migrants go to permanent or even temporary shelters, but they cannot stay for long periods, so if their situation does not improve, they still have to leave—that is, thousands of Mexican deportees who have lived in the US their entire lives and have no family in Mexico anymore. Sometimes their children stay back there or have their life sorted there and would not come back.

In February 2017, I visited migrant shelters to document hundreds of migrants' arrival in Tijuana. There were Mexican women escaping cartels and gender-based violence, as well as Guatemalans, Hondurans, and Salvadorians fleeing Central America's unceasing gang violence. There were also less likely suspects: Haitians who sought refuge in Brazil after the 2010 earthquake in their home country but had to move on due to Brazil's profound economic and political crisis, which has dramatically reduced job availability. These Haitians are not necessarily typical "economic migrants"; many are engineers, physicians, and architects aged twenty to thirty.

Indeed, this little-known group makes up the bulk of migrants stranded in Tijuana. According to Tijuana migrant activist Soraya Vázquez, from the Comité Estratégico de Ayuda Humanitaria Tijuana, 6 Haitians arrived in Tijuana on May 23, 2016. The next day there were 100. By early 2017, some 18,000 Haitians had entered the country, but by late 2018, only 3,500 were distributed in Tijuana, Baja California, and the state's capital Mexicali. They tried to get asylum in the US, but they tried to stay in Mexico as they failed. Church-run shelters helped them get jobs and build homes (Redacción El Heraldo de México 2018). By mid-2019, there were some 4,000 Haitians in Baja California claiming regular migratory status. Most Haitians arrive in Tijuana by way of Brazil, apparently through the trafficking network discussed before. In comparison, 10,000 Syrians have applied for asylum in the US during the same period. Asylum seekers cannot legally work, have no permanent residence, and, if they are Haitian, often do not speak Spanish.

Nevertheless, they must support themselves and their families while waiting for US immigration officials to figure out whether or when their asylum applications can be granted. Haitians lived in Tijuana's open-air garbage dumps, sewer systems, and around improvised migrant shelters. Many sought menial jobs on the black market, cleaning houses and offices, working in sweatshops, or delivering pizzas for as little as US$1.30 a day. In Tijuana in 2016, Haitians lived in precarious homes at El Bordo, a dried channel of the Tijuana River, next to the US border, and already dwelled by the homeless and drug addicts (Aviña Cerecer 2020). These homes were metal foil, fabric, and plastic waste (ñongos) (40.9 percent), deep holes underground (2.2 percent), sewer systems (19.2 percent), bridges (18 percent), and slopes (13 percent). Local authorities evicted them in 2016 and eventually settled and formed a 3,000-people community. Middle-class, educated Haitians have opened up small businesses such as restaurants, have married Mexicans, and enrolled in University programs, melting in Tijuana's cosmopolitan environment.

Hondurans have not been as lucky. When the caravan of between 7,000–15,000 people arrived in Tijuana in December 2018, they found a closed border; 100 of them tried to cross the line by force but were suppressed (Redacción BBC Mundo 2018). They have been the target of xenophobic attacks since the caravan arrived in late 2018, probably because they were not as educated and wealthy as Haitians or because they arrived when Europe shut down its borders, increasing migration flows through Africa and South America. In 2020, there are over 6,000 Hondurans in Tijuana, adding to a more massive crowd seeking asylum. Since the Remain in Mexico policy, thousands of migrants have returned. In April 2020, there were 10,000 people on waiting lists, and 6,400 had to wait for their next hearing in Mexico (Kao and Lu 2019). Trump called these people "invaders" and sent the army to prevent them from crossing. By late 2018, the US had deported 28,218 Hondurans (Pradilla 2019b). In January 2019, over 2,500 Hondurans lived in precarious conditions, in shelters or the streets, without access to food and getting ill because of the weather conditions they are not used to—coming from tropical geography. They face extreme desert weather. They also faced organized and regular crime (Proceso Digital 2019). For example, on December 15, drug dealers robbed and killed two Honduran teenagers who refused to buy drugs. Thousands of Hondurans, Africans, and even Mexicans face terrible conditions and remain in a time and space limbo that becomes spatially framed by the city's edges, geographies that allow for invisibility and disposability.

Pockets of Disposability

In their comparative study of Tijuana and other two Mexican cities—Puebla and Monterrey—Marchand and Ortega Ramírez (2019) examined the impact of migration on urban transformation using the concept of "worlding cities." The idea refers to the bottom-up insertion of third-world cities into the global political economy through low-skilled migrations. They look at different populations in these cities, including Haitians in Tijuana, concluding that they produce and reproduce these cities with their economic activities and integration in the economy. However, Marchand and Ortega Ramírez fail to account for the role of precarity, homelessness, illness, and exploitation in these migration assemblages. Although the study claims to give a bottom-up view of the urban spatialization of migration in Tijuana, they neglect those places where illegal trade occurs, the marginalized areas where drugs, prostitution, and other illegal services are offered (Marchand and Ortega Ra 2019).

Del Monte-Madrigal (2019) is more realistic about Tijuana and its possible generalization to similar places, calling it a "precarity vortex." As the result of an ethnographic study in the Mexican border city of Tijuana, he defines precarity vortex as "an enveloping set of spatial-temporal processes, made up of forces violent and exclusive sociocultural, which recursively structure the degradation progressive and exponential of the material, social and subjective conditions for subsistence" (Del Monte Madrigal 2018: 13). He observed different types of "constellations of precarity" that show interrelated processes—at the macro, middle, and micro levels—linking subjects' experiences and backgrounds with homelessness and structural processes in the border space. These constellations include "critical moments" such as deportation, family rupture, border limbo, and drug consumption, but also structural determinants such as deportation and migration. According to Del Monte Madrigal:

> Each of these precarious constellations begins in a precarious context and goes through a process of transnational mobility that crosses the border multiple times (represented by a thick blue line) and in whose coming and going there is a progressive accumulation of precariousness due to a conjunction of structural and subjective processes such as the reinforcement of the border, the tightening of migration policies, the condition of secrecy, involvement in drug use and incarceration processes. (Del Monte Madrigal 2018: 41)

Del Monte Madrigal's conceptualization of the precarity vortexes is robust since it builds on profound ethnographic observation and understanding of life in extreme precarity spaces. However, it lacks a global view of the role of law in creating such spaces. Precarity vortexes clearly describe the "centripetal" structural forces that gradually lead migrants to dwell in precarious urban spaces, such as migration processes, violence, and discrimination. However, the concept lacks an examination of the role of migration and asylum laws and policies in constructing these spaces, especially the managerial view of asylum justice and the presidential executive actions discussed in the previous section.

Analyzing the structural role of law in defining precarity spaces allows for identifying what Soja terms the "political organization of space." Soja's idea of spatial (in)justice contends that wealth and poverty are geographically distributed along the lines of class, race, and gender. These forces determine what he calls "spatial injustice," which is "created through the biases imposed on certain populations because of their geographical location" (Soja 2009: 3). For him, this phenomenon is "locational discrimination" that is "created through the biases imposed on certain populations because of their geographical location," and it "is fundamental in the production of spatial injustice and the creation of lasting spatial structures of privilege and advantage" (Soja 2009: 3). While Soja's examples range from the law for urban apartheid, residential segregation, and militarization, I contend that national borders and the laws defining mobility, such as asylum, deportation, and visas, are critical in creating spaces of injustice. The American asylum system and the more recent *pro morituri* asylum law and policy create locational discrimination of refugees, deportees, and global migrants in border cities such as Tijuana.

However, locational discrimination is not enough to describe migration and asylum laws' extreme exclusion because the radicalization of poverty does not illustrate the restrictions and expectations that asylum and refugee systems impose on subjects' "forceful hope" (Elliot 2016). Chapter 1 argued that whereas capital accumulation through lucrative death is the structural component of the apparatus of necropolitical production and management of forced migration, forceful hope is the subjective element. Those who become stranded through deportation and asylum waiting lists are trapped in the centripetal forces of precarity vortexes but in the context of the interruption of their migration project where hope remains. Necropower dumps migrants, but it does not mean that they lost hope. Forceful hope keeps them trying to get a new life, even against *pro morituri* laws and policies. Even though they are no longer valuable, they await in *pockets of disposability*.

Pockets of disposability are receptacles for unwanted people—a world population surplus that nevertheless insists on living. They are the spatialization of what Henry A. Giroux calls the "machinery of disposability" (Giroux 2014: par. 2)—see chapter 1. Deportees, people forced to flee natural disasters, like Haitians, and unimaginable violence in their home countries, like Central Americans and Mexicans, become disposable. They are human clutter in Mexico's dumps and gutters, at the gateway to one of the world's wealthiest nations. Pockets of disposability are areas of spatial injustice where vulnerable populations defined along the lines of nationality, class, race, and gender are forced into inhumane living conditions and illegal labor markets with the tacit approval of necropower. They are a radicalized version of what sociologists call pockets of poverty, that is, neighborhoods where the extremely poor tend to be corralled into ghettos, even as prosperity grows all around them (Mohda et al. 2016). In the context of necrocapitalism, pockets of disposability are part of what Ruth Wilson Gilmore (2020) calls "geographies of racial capitalism," the creation of mass incarceration for the exploitation of blacks and other ethnic minorities for the reproduction of an economic system permanently favoring whites and subordinating minorities (Card 2019). Pockets of disposability are, in fact, open-air jails for disposable forced migrants who refuse to lose hope.

Pockets of Disposability around the World

Sadly, pockets of disposability are not exclusive of Tijuana or even the US-Mexico border. These places where the rich dispose of asylum seekers, deportees, and migrants, in general, are found all over the world. They are in places where desperation meets hope, such as Venezuela's borders with Colombia and Brazil. They are too in towns where wealthy countries export their migratory boundaries, cities such as Athens.

In Mexico, in addition to Tijuana, there is Ciudad Juárez, Chihuahua, one of the deadliest cities in the country, especially for women. Juárez has received 11,500 migrants, including Mexican deportees, Honduran asylum seekers, and Cubans (Rocío 2018). Only 850 of them are in shelters. As for the Venezuelan crisis, 95 percent of the 1.2 million migrants pass through Cúcuta, Colombia. They settle down on riverbanks and hills, in tiny paperboard houses or improvised tents, with no sanitary services whatsoever. People employed themselves in the informal sector and, if they are women or girls, in prostitution. Venezuelans also migrate to Brazil via Roraima, particularly the capital Boa Vista and the border town of Pacaraima. In Roraima, there are 13 shelters with 6,000 Venezuelans, including 500 people of the Warao—the indigenous group settled in the Orinoco gold mining arch. In Pacaraima, there are 1,500 living in the streets and 3,000 in Boa Vista. Like Hondurans and Haitians in Tijuana, Venezuelans in Pacaraima live in the streets and sleep rough in squares and parking lots. They have been the victims of xenophobic attacks from residents. Finally, in Athens, thousands of migrants get stuck here because of the European Union's asylum and migration directives, forcing Greece to receive their visa and asylum applications. Many of them have settled down in the anarchist neighborhood of Exarchia. Locals and migrants share spaces peacefully, but recently drug traffickers have taken the zone, and the government blames migrants.

CONCLUSIONS

This chapter examined necropowers' management of forced migration through three technologies: the transnational necropolitical nomospheres, the *pro morituri* asylum laws, and the construction of pockets of disposability. The shutdown of dangerous routes does not persuade forced migrants from fleeing but pushes them to dangerous routes that transnational networks of criminal gangs and individual smugglers make not safer but merely available. These routes are expensive, lengthy, and dangerous because of geographical complexity and channels of distribution of illegal commodities, such as drugs. Thousands of African, Asian, and Central and South American migrants—forced migrants as a disposable subject—die trying to reach North America devoured by dangerous fauna and geographies or the greed of smugglers and other criminals who kidnap and extort them. Besides, migrants who finally reach the borders of destination countries face increasing legal obstacles for their asylum claims, which is the only legal means for poor people to immigrate to wealthy nations. Migrants are subjected to legal technologies that force them to wait in the borderline for months, sometimes with no access to shelter, food, and minimum sanitary conditions, in pockets of disposability.

Necropowers in Europe and North America have shut down their borders and safe routes to conduce forced migrants from all over the world to a deathly geographical bottleneck where permanent irregularity and corruption allow for a transnational web of individual smugglers and criminal gangs. Criminals profit from smuggling fees, extortion for safe passage, protection racketeering, kidnapping, illegal trade in organs, and sexual and labor trafficking. This space is the transnational necropolitical nomosphere. There, migrants are dispossessed of everything, even their bodies, for commodification, as disposable commodities (Treviño 2020), as discussed in chapter 1. Migrants who make it to the Mexico-US border face *pro morituri asylum laws*, including the same ban to be on American soil to stand in their trial. While they are waiting in Mexican border cities, they are confined to radical precarity spaces I call pockets of disposability. These places concentrate deprivation, illness, and violence in contained geographical areas within border cities or border enclaves trapping migrants within because they have no legal status.

NOTES

1. Since the early nineteenth century the US has used the law to keep away unwanted nonwhite and nonprotestant migrants such the Chinese, the Irish and Mexicans. However, the criminalization of immigration began with the Immigration

Reform and Control Act, or Simpson-Rodino Law, of 1986, which gave amnesty to three million undocumented workers, two million of them with Mexican nationality. At the same time it imposed sanctions on employers and increased monitoring of the border by doubling the number of border agents. In addition, at the federal level the 1996 Illegal Immigration Reform and Immigrant Responsibility Act focused on eliminating the access of undocumented immigrants to State social services on the basis of the false premise that the social security system was the principal attraction for undocumented immigrants. In California, Proposal 187—approved but then revoked by a federal court in 1994—attempted to prohibit the access of undocumented immigrants to public education and free medical services, except in the case of an emergency, in order to dissuade these immigrants from entering US territory. It also simplified the appeals process for deportation cases and authorized an increase in border patrol agents and immigration agents for the investigation of employers to document fraud and to document persons remaining in the country once their visas had expired. The greatest impact of this failed legislation was its influence at the federal level since it served as the inspiration for the Personal Responsibility and Work Opportunity Reconciliation Act, also of 1996, which denied undocumented migrants to access to public social services and increased financial and human resources for border monitoring. In addition, this Act increased sanctions for the trafficking of immigrants, punished the falsification of documents and facilitated deportations by eliminating audiences.

2. In December 2009 President Barack Obama established that asylum seekers able to prove "credible fear" of persecution by the government of their country, or by a group the government did not want to control or was unable to control, could remain in US territory until such time as the process for the asylum application was completed.

3. Legal clinics appealed many of these decisions, winning some cases like the suspension of DACA. See: Penn State Law. 2020. "Immigration in the Time of Trump." Penn State Law, accessed July 10, 2020. https://pennstatelaw.psu.edu/immigration-time-of-trump.

Conclusion

A Theorization of Forced Migration in the Necropolitical Era (Plus COVID-19)

Bringing examples and cases from several parts of the world but mainly the US border with Mexico, Central America, and South America, the book argued that forced migration is not a spontaneous phenomenon. People do not become migrants all of a sudden. Necropower in the third world *produces* migration with development projects, mineral and resource exploitation, the trade of illicit commodities ranging from drugs to organs and sex, and the instrumentalization of organized crime and violence for these purposes. Then first world necropower *manages* forced depopulation, employing legal categories such as the refugee and asylum, which neoliberal governmentality of migration has subsumed, producing discourses of forced migration and categories that lack rights content. In order to carry out this analytical research, I employed a Foucaultian methodology based on the analysis of forced migration as an apparatus deploying strategies of production and administration. I employed a genealogical approach to examine the postcolonial analysis of the link between the historical asylum regime and the contemporary global migration governance.

The book's objective was to theorize forced migration from a necropolitics perspective. It argued that forced migration is a process in which a set of legal and illegal policies, laws, institutions, political discourses, and markets produce death gains. The necropolitical process of forced migration is based on the gradual construction of bureaucratic apparatuses, discourses, policies, and strategies that guarantee that poor and racialized people, considered disposable (Treviño 2020), cease to be obstacles to extractivist capitalism and hyperconsumption. The apparatus uses political and criminal terror to kill the communities that oppose them and leave asylum seekers to die using international law and policy.

I borrowed from Achille Mbembe's necropolitics to suggest two types of necropower inducing and administration migration: the necropolitical governmentalization of the State in the third world and the rule of law necropower in the first world. Regarding the former, I argued that the necropolitical governmentalization of the State implies the delegation of technologies of domination—the means of coercion—to criminal gangs for control of the population through murder, torture, persecution, human trafficking, and sex trafficking. It uses political discourses such as the war on drugs or the security crisis to regulate death, the securitization of public spaces as the central strategy, and the criminal economy as the primary motivation. The actors of the necropolitical governmentalization of the State include drug cartels, gangs, politicians, some sectors of the army, police, and even first world governments financing the war on drugs and promoting mining and agricultural corporations. Death in the necropolitical governmentality of the State is productive in the sense that the knowledge and technologies of death are a valuable commodity for the production of situations of terror and chaos that eventually favor the extractive activities of corporations.

As for the rule of law necropower, it is the sovereignty to administer death through adherence to the rule of law and the neocolonial spatiality that it creates or emphasizes not simply to discipline or annihilate racialized bodies to profit from their death or the conditions that eventually lead to death. It is the application of the rule of law for the subjectivation and creation of spaces of coloniality that reproduce capital from the criminalization that leads to confinement and hatred, the abandonment that leads to the use of drugs and diseases, and the poisoning and erosion of habitats that lead to adverse and chronic health conditions.

I argue that necropower in rich countries and their global institutions is the sovereign power to kill along the lines of class, race, ethnicity, nationality, gender, and class, not within states of exception but under the rule of law. I called this first world necropower the necropower of the rule of law because first world countries and the institutions of global governance they control claim to guide their actions with the legal principles of the rule of law: accountability, just laws, open government, accessible justice. The policies and decisions of the first world necropower may not be fair or humane, but they are always legal. In the first world and its institutions, necropower works not above or below the law but through it. The rule of law necropower leads to deathly situations, such as the deportation of refugees and fortifying secure borders. Dying is legal. The rule of law necropower is the sovereignty to administer death through adherence to the rule of law and the neocolonial spatiality that it creates or emphasizes not simply to discipline or annihilate racialized bodies but to profit from their death or the conditions that eventually lead to death. It is the application of the rule of law for the subjectivation and creation of spaces of coloniality that reproduce capital from the criminalization that leads to confinement and hatred, the abandonment that leads to the use of drugs and diseases, and the poisoning and erosion of habitats that leads to adverse and chronic health conditions.

Forced migration is the residual result of two strategies that the necropowers use to dispose of people who inhabit geographies rich in renewable and nonrenewable natural resources while benefiting from deadly technologies such as criminal and gang, sexual and gender violence, which produce the death of men and women differently. These strategies are forced depopulation (extractive activities focused on mining, fracking, and logging) and lucrative death (criminal violence that benefits from lucrative death, violence that commercializes the threat of annihilation of human bodies). Together or separately, these strategies produce forced migration.

On the one hand, forced depopulation is the necropolitical strategy that has the purpose of inhabiting geographies rich in renewable and nonrenewable natural resources for their exploitation. Forced migration is just one of the many forms used to depopulate geographies rich in natural resources, mainly hydrocarbons and minerals. The necropower that operates here includes the political-economic oligarchies and transnational corporations based in those countries. It is a process that begins with structural and accumulation projects, often facilitated by the police or organized crime activities, which displace or ultimately kill people. Forcibly displaced persons are more exposed to gangs, organized crime, and sexual violence while in transit.

On the other hand, lucrative death results from murders generated by the reproduction of extractive capitalism and the markets for illegal goods. It is perpetrated by necro-empowered subjects who are both objects and subjects of neoliberalism. Extractivism and illegal markets, on the one hand, and necro-empowered subjects, on the other, are the structural and subjective factors that produce lucrative death and capital accumulation. Lucrative death is productive both in terms of capital and the constitutive nature of necro-capitalist practices. It occurs in a political economy of illegal drugs, where criminals can use this infrastructure to trade commercialized human lives: trafficking and smuggling of people, sex, and the trade in organs, among others. This economy generates a continuum in which criminal and sexual violence is part of a continuum of colonial, gender, and racialized violence to secure criminal markets and the commodification of women's bodies while producing forced migration in the context of forced depopulation.

Once the conditions are in place for forced migration to exist, the necropowers of the rule of law lead migrants through geographies of death where a network of necropolitical states allow criminal gangs to smuggle, traffic, extort, and, ultimately, kill forced migrants. Those who do not die on the way have to face asylum and migration systems of the necropowers of the rule of law under the necropolitical pro morituri legal principle. In this way, the necropolitical administration of migration contains three strategies: the transnational necropolitical spatialization of the international asylum and migration regime; the application of *pro morituri* asylum laws through national asylum systems; and the eviction of deported migrants and migrants and future refugees in disposable pockets.

Firstly, the rule of law necropower creates permanently irregular legal spaces that facilitate lucrative death. Many of the legal spaces function according to state borders and function differently in the first and third world. However, the spatialization of law in the administration of forced migration is transnational. The transnational necropolitical spatialization of law is the organized space for regulating lucrative death through a network of permanently irregular, corrupt, and functional national legal systems at death. It is a network of necropolitical national legal systems that instrumentalize impunity, crime, and environmental conditions for the lucrative death of migrants.

Secondly, one of the characteristics of the necropower of the rule of law is the legal formalism interpreted with the pro morituri principle. Legal formalism refers to how legal reasoning and dispute resolution inform a liberal system of legal deduction. It requires basic principles in a given area of law and resolving the dispute through deductive reasoning based on the initial principles. Liberal legal discourses highlight the importance of individuality and life when interpreting law under the customary pro persona principle—interpreting the law to provide the most significant benefit to legal subjects. Instead, the necropower of the rule of law adheres to legal formalism but legislates and interprets the norms through a necropolitical legal principle that I call pro morituri, the legal interpretation that prioritizes legal conditions that lead to death and not to the most outstanding protection for the individual. The rule of law necropower legislates and interprets the law through norms and policies that lead people to deadly scenarios, such as laws that facilitate deportation, closure of borders and militarization, mass expulsions, child vulnerability due to family separation, and exposure to disease and violence.

Finally, disposability pockets are receptacles for the unwanted, a surplus of the world's population that nonetheless insists on living. They are the spatialization of human disposability. The deported, people forced to flee natural disasters, and violence unimaginable in their home countries become disposable. They are human waste in the dumps and gutters of the borders between the third and first world. Pockets of disposability are areas of spatial injustice where vulnerable populations defined by nationality, class, race, and gender are forced to live in inhuman conditions and with illegal labor markets with the tacit approval of the necropower. They are a radicalized version of what sociologists call "pockets of poverty," that is, neighborhoods where the extremely poor tend to be cornered in ghettos, even as prosperity grows around them, in the context of necro-capitalism. Disposability pockets are, in effect, open-air prisons for disposable forced migrants who refuse to give up hope.

This new necropolitical framework for the analysis of forced migration reveals the postcolonial power issues underlying the making of migration itself. At the same time, it shows how law and policy are used for the administration of migration as a postcolonial administration of racialized people living in impoverished geographies rich in natural resources. The necropolitical apparatus for the production and administration of forced migration offers a set of new concepts—forced depopulation, lucrative death, pro morituri laws, necropolitical nomospheres, disposability pockets—that can help researchers to observe death administration in postcolonial spaces as different as a rural community and a supranational organization such as the United Nations. Further research could focus on the specificities of gender law and policy producing and administrating migration. Also, further research could expand the scope of analytical tools to examine migration production and management in the context of COVID-19. While writing the book, a world-changing event took place: the COVID-19 epidemics. Too soon to analyze the implications of the pandemics on forced migration, and too late to include COVID-19 throughout the book, I could only offer a thread of analysis for further investigation for other researchers to pick.

WHAT FUTURE FOR HUMAN MOBILITY AFTER COVID-19?

Starting with the idea that necropowers produce and manage migration spatially and with race and class criteria, I contend that further investigation should start by looking at what happened with the previous pandemics in terms of class and race and look at how the COVID-19 pandemic enables a hierarchy of mobility according to class and race.

Virologist Luc Montagnier, who won the Nobel Prize for his research on HIV, said there is a remarkable similarity between SARS-CoV-2, the cause of COVID-19, and HIV, the cause of AIDS. Since both viruses attack the immune system, the scientist even claims that the new coronavirus was created in a laboratory by grafting HIV into a coronavirus. Of course, this assertion has gone into the pantheon of the various conspiracy theories that have emerged around the pandemic threatening the civilization model known as globalization. It may be that the biochemistry of both viruses is not the same and they do not have any biological connection, but the truth is that, like the most significant pandemics of the last fifty years, both have similarities in their social and discursive construction, in how we assign them bodies and materiality.

HIV/Aids, we know, emerged in the early 1980s, attacking men who had sex with other men first, and then other groups that stigmatized the spread: drug users and hemophiliacs. The first person to get infected with HIV was a man in Africa who ate chimpanzee meat; chimpanzees are carriers of a similar virus called the simian immunodeficiency virus. So far, HIV/Aids has killed 35 million people all over the world. However, in its early stages, HIV was widespread among gay men and drug users led to the biased and prejudiced idea that it was a disease of gay and drug users. This idea permeated the world's imagination for a long time, making its diagnosis, treatment, and social visibility very difficult and shameful in a hetero-patriarchal world.

The SARS-CoV-2/COVID-19, for its part, received this name so as not to stigmatize nationalities in the way that the Spanish or Chinese influenza previously did. The new coronavirus emerged in the Chinese city of Wuhan so that the stigma was easy to establish. The first carriers of SARS-CoV-2/COVID-19 to the West were travelers, middle-class, and wealthy people; the first cases were among middle-class people returning from vacation in Europe and skiing resorts in the US. However, it is likely that its contagion will eventually stigmatize migration because SARS-CoV-2/COVID-19 is associated with human mobility—from the very departure from home without a mouthpiece to a vacation trip or migration due to violence, poverty, and now illness. Mobility will be the new "unsafe sex." However, let us not forget that mobility control has always been associated with at least two characteristics: class and race, and within these, gender can deepen stigmatization experiences. The "infectious" bodies will be those of forced migrants. We shall face a double standard for mobility. The already called digital nomads of what I called elsewhere zoomism (Estévez 2020) might have the means to move more freely. Wealthy travelers and tourists will likely carry vaccine records or even biological passports. In contrast, forced migrants will be the potentially COVID-19 carriers, the "walking waste" whose low-skilled jobs and expertise require them to move and seek opportunities where "essential jobs" are offered.

ZOOMISM

In a short article, I wrote that for the middle classes around the world, mobility control started through what I called zoomism. There were shocking images of New York and Venice's deserted cities, which showed that the discipline of self-confinement was eventually successful. As Foucault pointed out in the case of school and the army, we resisted discipline—but in the end, we confined ourselves to the home as an institution of isolation for biopolitical purposes. Since going out and seeing others put them and us at risk, it made us accept and organize work meetings and school classes online. Even talking to friends was dangerous, so we resorted to online meeting platforms. A few months ago, few people knew about the Zoom platform. Today everyone uses it. At this point in quarantine, various platforms facilitate meetings for office work, business, politics, and school, but for analytical purposes, let us say that Zoom establishes the production model for which we are being disciplined. We are facing a change in the importance of the transition from Fordism to Toyotaism. This change aims to immobilize us sufficiently to control human mobility—the human virus that has destroyed the planet—without bringing production and consumption to a halt. A microeconomy of self-enclosure is already in place: zoomism.

Self-enclosure is a technology for disciplining bodies for the government of mobility, permitting the same rhythm of consumption and growth for production and markets, the sectors that sustain current neoliberalism (mining extractivism for the digital industry and bio-work for the production of big data) without continued damage to the planet, which is now a source of natural resources rather than life itself. The objective is not to stop economic production or consumption, but rather human mobility, to change lifestyles.

We face the disciplining of bodies as part of global biopolitics to change the working model and limit the elite's mobility. The global middle classes are not going to be treated that way. They can be left to die, but they will not be directed to death scenarios like forced migrants who drown in the Mediterranean or are swallowed by the jungles of the Darien Gap between Colombia and Panama. For the middle classes, there is self-enclosure to guarantee immobility. The anatomo-politics—as Michel Foucault named the techniques of disciplining bodies to make them docile and manipulable—of self-enclosure serves to curtail the middle classes' mobility that travel for tourism business, academic conferences, and trade relations. This segment of the population has the income to afford international flights and extreme experiences in the most remote places. Nevertheless, these same people are—we are—those who can work from the refuge of home using a virtual platform.

We know from Foucault that in governmentality, there is no necessary intention in the cause, or at least there is no direct intention; it is always the management of behaviors: inhibiting, procuring, annulling, reversing, manipulating, controlling, or assuring the actions of the other leading to self-care, self-regulation, or, in this case, self-imposed immobility. The critical thing about behavior management is productivity, the benefits it brings, and who benefits from them.

Fordism, as we know, was the model of mass industrial production that replaced Taylorism and guaranteed full employment and universal or employment-linked social security, as occurred in Mexico among other countries. Toyotaism, which replaced Fordism, established piece-rate, hourly work without compulsory social security. Zoomism would be the mode of production for self-enclosure, increasing added value since corporate offices' operating costs are transferred to workers: electricity, the internet, water, and even coffee. Without time to travel to work or even to venture outside, we become more productive. The current quarantine disciplines us to immobility, seclude our bodies, and project our professional avatars through digital platforms, reformulating the perception of time and space of globalization. David Harvey conceptualized this as the compression of space and time through information technology and low-cost flights that increased and changed tourism, business, and work. We will progress from a relative perception of global space-time as something compressed to space-time perception and experience in absolute terms: a materially immobile present and space that moves only virtually.

Zooming, of course, has a significant class component, just as the spread of COVID-19 did initially—tourists and travelers spread it around the world. This virus was propagated by ex-pats and foreigners, not by forced migrants. For the latter, the necropolitical device of production and administration of forced migration is still in place and will instrumentalize COVID-19 as it has administered other diseases and dangers. For them, it is business as usual. Change comes with disciplining the middle classes, who will self-regulate, giving up trips contributing to global warming and spreading viruses.

WALKING WASTE

We have already seen that the quarantine standstill has reduced carbon emissions in China. Immobility stops people, not the industries that sustain neoliberal capitalism. Here is where the management of migrants' death comes to play. The mobility of the most precarious, economic, and forced migrants has already been managed for some time, leading them to death in what the book calls the necropolitical apparatus of production and administration of forced migration. Amid the COVID-19 pandemics, necropower shall construct migration as potentially contaminated. Some biases are probably at play already: Venezuelan president Nicolás Maduro said in August 2020 that citizens returning from Colombia would be considered "bioterrorists" and called on people to accuse them before the authorities. Maduro apologized the next day, but it is a sign that COVID-19 will be associated with precarious mobility. Migrants' bodies will become toxic, similar to what Svetlana Alexievich's book *Voices of Chernobyl* refers to as "walking waste," that is, living beings whose bodies are so toxic that their bodies are not even useful for food.

The colonial, class, and race bias of the COVID-19 pandemic will continue how the virus migrated in the first place. In Latin America, the images of the bodies lying on the streets of Guayaquil, Ecuador, were shocking and painful. They lack the middle-class romanticism of the photos of empty Barcelona, Venice, and New York. The contrast of the empty streets in Europe and the United States and the dead in Ecuador's second-largest city's ditches is the crudest expression of the coloniality that constitutes migratory movements today. In an article, the Peruvian philosopher Aníbal Quijano explains that coloniality "is one of the constituents and specific elements of the world pattern of capitalist power. It is based on the imposition of a racial/ethnic classification of the world's population as the cornerstone of this pattern of power and operates on each of the material and subjective planes, fields, and dimensions of daily existence and a social scale" (Quijano 2007: 285).

Quijano's coloniality of power repeats itself in the spatialization of COVID-19 within the transnational nomosphere. The privileged classes of poor countries (tourists) took the virus with them when returning from their holidays in China, Spain, Italy, the US, and other European countries. Migrant workers in Europe also took the virus when returning to their home country for the winter holidays—Ecuadorians working in Spain, for instance. Ecuador is also a strategic space for global migration, as explained in chapter 4. In a heartbreaking article in which she describes and analyzes the pandemic's situation in Guayaquil, Ecuadorian academic María Fernanda Moscoso traced Case Zero, linking it to the Ecuadorian circular migration to Spain. She concludes that although Case Zero can be traced back to this circular migration, Guayaquil's tragedy has to do with the oligarchy and the class canons of those who went ahead with a party and brought the infection to the popular classes. The colonial-virus, she claims (Moscoso Rosero 2020).

However, the coloniality of COVID-19 goes far beyond the migration of the virus itself. It has to do with how death is managed. Therefore, in addition to crossing the Darien in Panama and Colombia and confronting traffickers like the Gulf Clan, they have to face the COVID-19 and the new challenges and scenarios: staying in shelters without any kind of protocol for the prevention of contagion; follow the path looking for smugglers made more expensive by the increased danger of the route and the quarantine or being stranded in border cities of extreme precariousness. However, given the space-time paradox of the need for mobility—to return home or continue the journey—and the immobility imposed by the pandemic—quarantine—the administration of death in forced migration produces mixed emotions that self-regulate the migrants to conduct themselves to death.

Since the first outbreaks of contagion occurred in South America last March, forced migrants on their way to the United States have faced unsanitary situations in shelters that have ended in fires and riots, such as in Tenosique, Mexico (Movimiento Migrante Mesoamericano 2020). Like those who have wanted to return from Italy, Spain, and the United States, African, Asian and Caribbean migrants became stranded in Panama and Honduras during the lockdown because the government shut down their borders. Migrants could not move for months (United Nations 2020, Refugees International 2020, AFP 2020).

However, the necropolitics of COVID-19 has its most potent expression on Mexico's border with the United States with the impasse in which President Donald Trump has put asylum with the worsening of the pandemic in the United States with which the pockets of disposability became increasingly deadly. Trump ordered the closure of its borders, even for minors. The United States deported all migrants without papers, including asylum seekers and minors, without checking if the principle of nonrefoulment was violated or if there are measures to prevent the virus from spreading the virus repatriation to Mexico, Honduras, Guatemala, and Ecuador if they are infected. The deportees now number more than 10,000. Mexico accepts its nationals and Central Americans, but there is no control or quick tests to determine if the deportees are carriers.

With the closure of borders and based on secure third country agreements, the colonial border of the United States can be found now in Central America, and those who want to leave their countries in search of refuge in the north are being detained. Those who manage to save the borders of the Central American region are detained on the southern border of Mexico, where the processing of asylum cases has been postponed indefinitely (by July 2020). Hundreds of asylum seekers have been detained at their immigration stations where they are quarantined in unsanitary and desperate situations, such as in a shelter in Tenosique, Tabasco, where fear of contagion caused a riot that resulted in a fire that resulted in a migrant's death. Likewise, Mexico is abandoning hundreds of deportees from the United States in the south of the country, without controlling the virus. Simultaneously, in border cities such as Tijuana, the situation worsens day by day and puts hundreds of migrants from all over the world at risk.

In summary, using Mexico and Central America, the United States is instrumentalizing COVID-19 to accelerate the death of forced migrants from all over the world, in border cities and other places of great inequality and precariousness where life was hardly possible. Consequently, in March 2020, the Centers for Disease Control issued an order prohibiting people's entry from "areas affected by the coronavirus," giving the Border Patrol the power to deport people who arrive at the border without giving them the chance to apply for asylum. By April 2020, nearly 21,000 people had been deported as a result of this new policy. As stated above, all MPP hearings at the border and asylum cooperation agreements were suspended. As a result, the asylum process has been completely blocked for people arriving at the United States-Mexico border during COVID-19.

Bibliography

ACLU San Diego. 2018. "End Zero Tolerance and Operation Streamline Now." American Civil Liberties Union ACLU San Diego, accessed April 6, 2018. https://www.aclusandiego.org/operationstreamline/.

ACNUR. 2016. Tendencias globales: Desplazamiento forzado en 2015. Ginebra: Alto Comisionado de las Naciones Unidas para los Refugiados.

ACNUR. 2017. Tendencias globales: Desplazamiento forzado en 2016. Ginebra: ACNU.

AFP. 2020. Policía hondureña frena migración de africanos hacia México. *France24*.

Agamben, Giorgio. 1998. *Homo sacer. El poder soberano y la nuda vida.* España: Pre-textos.

Agamben, Giorgio. 2001. *Medios sin fin*. España: Pre-textos.

Agamben, Giorgio. 2004. *El estado de excepción.* Archipiélago.

Agamben, Giorgio. 2009. *What is an apparatus? And other essays*. Stanford, California: Stanford University Press.

Álvarez, Priscila. 2019. Confusion and frustration in tent courts along the Texas border. *CNN Politics* (September 21, 2019): https://edition.cnn.com/2019/09/21/politics/texas-tent-courts/index.html.

Álvarez, Priscila. 2020a. Appeals court pauses its ruling that dealt major blow to administration's immigration agenda. *CNN Politics* (February 29, 2020): https://edition.cnn.com/2020/02/28/politics/asylum-seekers-mexico-appeals-court/index.html. Accessed July 10, 2020.

Álvarez, Priscila. 2020b. 'I don't want to be deported': Inside the tent courts on the US-Mexico border. *CNN Politics* (January 28, 2020): https://edition.cnn.com/2020/01/28/politics/tent-courts-remain-in-mexico/index.html?fbclid=IwAR2odjG3Z6iF-AVN6X219CA_NBStDarXAfbDfUcckMVn3e9wrVeMn7nWhws. Accessed July 10, 2020.

Álvarez Velasco, Soledad. 2016. "Human smugglers roundtable: Soledad Alvarez Velasco." Open Democracy. https://www.opendemocracy.net/en/beyond-trafficking-and-slavery/human-smugglers-roundtable-soledad-alvarez-velasco/.

Andersen, Bridget. 2014. "Trafficking." In *The Oxford Handbook of Refugee and Forced Migration Studies*, edited by Elena Fiddian-Qasmiyeh, Gil Loescher, Kat Long, and Nando Sigona. Oxford: Oxford University Press.

Anderson, Ben. 2012. "Affect and biopower: towards a politics of life." *Transactions of the Institute of British Geographers*

Anzilotti, Eillie. 2017. Refugee Camps Are Turning Into Permanent Cities–Can They Be Smart Cities? *FastCompany* (July 19, 2017).

Aviña Cerecer, Gustavo. 2020. "The Dispossessed of Necropolitics on the San Diego-Tijuana Border." *Social Sciences* 9 (6):15.

Bakewell, Oliver. 2008. "Research Beyond the Categories: The Importance of Policy Irrelevant Research into Forced Migration." *Journal of Refugee Studies* 21: (432–453).

Balibar, Etienne, Sandro Mezzadra, and Ranabir Samaddar. 2012. *The borders of justice*. Philadelphia: Temple University Press.

Banerjee, Bobby. 2008. "Necrocapitalism." *Organization Studies:* 1541–1563.

Bargent, James, and cat Rainsford. 2020. GameChangers 2019: minería ilegal, economía criminal en auge. *Analysis* 2020 (August 27, 2020).

Bastos, Cristiana. 2008. "Migrants, Settlers and Colonists: The Biopolitics of Displaced Bodies." *International Migration* 46 (5):27–54.

Battistessa, Diego. 2019. Una masacre silenciosa: las venezolanas muertas en el extranjero. *El País*: https://elpais.com/elpais/2019/09/02/planeta_futuro/1567434636_760205.html.

Baum, Dan. 2016. Legalize it all: How to win the war on drugs. *Harper's Magazine*.

BBC Latin America and the Caribbean. 2014. Who is behind Mexico's drug-related violence? (February 10, 2014): http://www.bbc.com/news/world-latin-america-10681249.

BBC Latin America and the Caribbean. 2020. De qué países de América Latina son los refugiados que hacen de España la nación con más solicitudes de asilo de la Unión Europea. BBC, News Mundo, 5. *BBC News Mundo*.

Berlant, Lauren. 2011. *Cruel optimism*. Durham and London: Duke University Press.

Bessi, Renata, and Santiago Navarro F. 2015. Fracking Expands in Latin America, Threatening to Contaminate World's Third-Largest Aquifer. *Truthout* (December 6, 2015): http://www.truth-out.org/news/item/33910-fracking-expands-in-latin-america-threatening-to-contaminate-world-s-third-largest-aquifer.

Betts, Alexander. 2010. "The Refugee Regime Complex." *Refugee Survey Quarterly*, 29 (1):12–37.

Bhagat, Ali H. 2018. "Queer necropolitics of forced migration: Cyclical violence in the African context." *Sexualities* 23 (3):361–375.

Bhatia, Monish. 2020. "The Permission to be Cruel: Street-Level Bureaucrats and Harms Against People Seeking Asylum." *Critical Criminology*. DOI: https://doi.org/10.1007/s10612-020-09515-3.

Bigo, Didier. 2002. "Security and Immigration: Toward a Critique of the Governmentality of Unease." *Alternatives: Global, Local, Political* 27 (1):63–92.

Black, Richard. 2001. "Fifty Years of Refugee Studies: From Theory to Policy." *The International Migration Review* 35 (1):57–78.

Boadle, Anthony. 2020. U.S. backs program to settle Venezuelan migrants in Brazil. *Reuters* (January 28, 2020): https://www.reuters.com/article/us-venezuela-brazil-usa/u-s-backs-program-to-help-venezuelan-migrants-settle-in-brazil-idUSKBN1ZR2I8#:~:text=Of%20the%204.6%20million%20Venezuelans,day%2C%20the%20Brazilian%20government%20says. Accessed August 27, 2020.

Bolaños, Bernardo. 2009. "Migración, derecho consular y justicia global." *Isonomía: Revista de teoría y filosofía del derecho* (30):7–30.

Bonello, Deborah. 2019. From Africa to Mexico. How far would you go for the American dream? *The Telegraph* (https://www.telegraph.co.uk/news/african-migrants-in-america/).

Bonnett, Gill. 2017. Climate change refugee cases rejected. *RadioNZ*. Accessed Novemeber 16, 2018.

Borton, John, and Sarah Collinson. 2017. Responses to mixed migration in Europe: Implications for the humanitarian sector. London: Humanitarian Practice Network (HPN).

Boycott UAE Team. 2017. Press Release: Human Trafficking in Dubai on the rise. *Boycott UAE*. Accessed November 16, 2018.

Bruin, Roland HM. 2002. "Working Party on Non-State Agents of Persecution: 2002 Report." In *5th Conference of the International Association of Refugee Law Judges. Stemming the tide or keeping the balance:the role of the judiciary*, edited by International Association of Refugee Law Judges, 451–464. Wellington New Zealand: International Association of Refugee Law Judges.

Buchanan, Holly. 2010. "Fleeing the Drug War Next Door: Drug-related Violence as a Basis for Refugee Protection for Mexican Asylum-Seekers." *Merkourios. Utrecht Journal of International and European Law* 27 (72):28–60.

Butler, Judith, and Athena Athanasiou. 2013. *Dispossession: the performative in the political*. Malden, MA: Polity.

Çam, Deniz. 2019. "Here's The Company Behind Trump's Controversial Border 'Tent Courts' For Migrants." *Forbes*.

Campesi, Giuseppe. 2012. "Migraciones, seguridad y confines en la teoría social contemporánea." *Revista Crítica Penal y Poder* 2012 (3):1–66.

Card, Kenton. 2019. Geographies of Racial Capitalism with Ruth Wilson Gilmore. US: BFD Productions.

Carens, Joseph. 2013. *The ethics of immigration*. New York: Oxford University Press.

Castillo, Milton. 2018. Iván Roa: "Ecuador dejó de ser un país de paz desde hace mucho tiempo." *Ecuadortoday* (June 2018).

CEAV. 2016. Resultados preliminares del Diagnóstico sobre la atención de la violencia sexual en México-resumen ejecutivo. México: Comisión Ejecutiva de Atención a Víctimas.

Center for Migration Studies. 2020. "President Trump's executive orders on immigration and refugees." Center for Migration Studies, accessed July 10, 2020. https://cmsny.org/trumps-executive-orders-immigration-refugees/.

CESPAD. 2018. *Hidroeléctricas y minería: la corrupción desde el Estado, detrás de las concesiones*.

Chaparro, Maria Paula Chaparro. 2019. Human Smuggling from Asia to Latin America On Rise. *Insight Crime Briefs* (November 12, 2019).

Chavkin, Sasha. 2015. Bathed In Blood. World Bank's Business-Lending Arm Backed Palm Oil Producer Amid Deadly Land War. *Huffington Post* (June 9, 2015). Accessed November 16, 2018.

Chayes, Sarah. 2017. When Corruption is the Operating System: The Case of Honduras. Washington DC: Carnegie Endowment for International Peace.

Chimni, Bhupinder. 1998. "The Geopolitics of Refugee Studies: A View from the South." *Journal of Refugee Studies* 11 (4):350–374.

Chimni, Bhupinder. 2009. "The birth of a discipline: from refugee to forced migration studies." *Journal of Refugee Studies:* 11–29.

CNDH. 2016. Informe Especial sobre Desplazamiento Forzado Interno (DFI) en México. México: Comisión Nacional de Derechos Humanos.

Cohen, Corentin. 2019. "Development of the Brazilian Drug Market Toward Africa: Myths, Evidence and Theoretical Questions." *Journal of Illicit Economies and Development* 1 (2):134–144.

Coles, Gervase. 1989. "Approaching the Refugee Problem Today." In *Refugees and International Relations*, edited by Gil Loescher and Laila Monahan, 442. London: Clarendon Press.

Contra Corriente. 2019. "Especial: al sur del sol: Corrupción en proyectos fotovoltaicos expulsa a gente del sur." https://contracorriente.red/2019/09/18/sol-de-sobra-y-falta-de-energia-por-corrupcion/.

Correa-Cabrera, Guadalupe. 2015. "Desigualdades y flujos globales en la frontera noreste de México: los efectos de la migración, el comercio, energéticos y crimen organizado transnacional." *Canadian Journal of Latin American and Caribbean Studies* 40 (3):326–350.

Correa-Cabrera, Guadalupe. 2018. *Los Zetas Inc.* México: Temas de hoy.

CPI. 1998. Estatuto de Roma de la Corte Penal Internacional, edited by Corte Penal Internacional. Roma: ONU.

Davies, T. and A. Isakjee (2019). "Ruins of Empire: Refugees, race and the postcolonial geographies of European migrant camps." *Geoforum* 102(2019): 214–217.

Davies, T., A. Isakjee and S. Dhesi (2017). "Violent Inaction: The Necropolitical Experience of Refugees in Europe." *Antipode* 49(5):1263–1284.

De Genova, Nicholas. 2010. "The Deportation Regime: Sovereignty, Space, and the Freedom of Movement." In *Theoretical Overview. The Deportation Regime: Sovereignty, Space, and the Freedom of Movement*, edited by Nicholas De Genova and Nathalie Peutz. Durham: Duke University Press.

De Vogue, Ariane. 2020. US Supreme Court lets 'Remain in Mexico' asylum policy stays in place. *CNN Politics* (March 11): https://edition.cnn.com/2020/03/11/politics/supreme-court-remain-in-mexico/index.html. Accessed July 10, 2020.

Dehm, Sara. 2020. "International Law at the Border: Refugee Deaths, the Necropolitical State and Sovereign Accountability." In *Routledge Handbook of International Law and the Humanities*, edited by Shane Chalmers and Sundhya Pahuja. Routledge.

Del Monte Madrigal, Juan Antonio. 2018. “El vórtice de precarización. El proceso de indigencia en una ciudad fronteriza del norte de México.” Doctor en Sociaología, El Colegio de México.

Delaney, David. 2010. *The spatial, the legal and the pragmatics of world-making: nomospheric investigations*. London: Routledge.

Delgado Mahecha, Ovidio. 2003. *Debates sobre el espacio en la geografía contemporánea*. Bogotá: Universidad Nacional de Colombia.

Department of Homeland Security. 2019a. Interim Final Rule on Asylum Eligibility and Procedural Modifications. Edited by Department of Homeland Security’s Executive Office for Immigration Review. Washington, DC: https://s3.amazonaws.com/public-inspection.federalregister.gov/2019-15246.pdf.

Department of Homeland Security. 2019b. Interim Final Rule on Implementing Bilateral and Multilateral Asylum Cooperative Agreements Under the Immigration and Nationality Act. Edited by Department of Homeland Security’s Executive Office for Immigration Review. Washington, DC: https://s3.amazonaws.com/public-inspection.federalregister.gov/2019-25137.pdf?utm_medium=email&utm_campaign=pi+subscription+mailing+list&utm_source=federalregister.gov.

Department of Homeland Security. 2019c. Migrant Protection Protocols. Edited by Homeland Security. Washington DC Department of Homeland Security.

Department of State. 2020. “Mexico Travel Advisory.” https://travel.state.gov/content/travel/en/traveladvisories/traveladvisories/mexico-travel-advisory.html.

Dixon, Laura, Pedro Noel, Andrea Arzaba, Sally Hayden, Mauro Pimentel, and Selase Kove-Seyram. 2018. Latin American Smugglers are now trafficking asylum seekers from across the globe. *Pacific Standard* (January 4, 2018): https://psmag.com/social-justice/asylum-seekers-are-turning-to-latin-american-smugglers.

Domenech, Eduardo. 2018. “Gobernabilidad migratoria: producción y circulación de una categoría de intervención política.” *Revista Temas de Antropología y Migración* (10):110–118.

Dussel, Enrique. 2005. “Transmodernidad e Interculturalidad: Interpretación desde la Filosofía de la Liberación.” In *La colonialidad del saber: Eurocentrismo y ciencias sociales*, edited by Edgardo Lander. Buenos Aires: Unesco, Ciccus, Clacso.

Elliot, Alice. 2016. “Forceful hope.” AllegraLab, London.

Estévez, Ariadna. 2013. “The Politics Of Death In Mexico: Dislocating Human Rights And Asylum Law Through Hybrid Agents.” *Glocalism: Journal of Culture, Politics and Innovation* 1 (1):1–28.

Estévez, Ariadna. 2016a. Fracking, mining, murder: the killer agenda driving migration in Mexico and Central America. *The Conversation Global* (November 23, 2016): https://theconversation.com/fracking-mining-murder-the-killer-agenda-driving-migration-in-mexico-and-central-america-67822.

Estévez, Ariadna. 2016b. Latin American women’s problem: we keep getting murdered .*The Conversation Global* (October 26, 2016): https://theconversation.com/latin-american-womens-problem-we-keep-getting-murdered-67351.

Estévez, Ariadna. 2017. “La repolitización los derechos humanos frente a la gubernamentalidad neoliberal del sufrimiento social: una lucha de contraconducta.” In

9 razones para (des)confiar de las luchas por los derechos humanos, edited by Ariadna Estévez and daniel Vázquez. México: UNAM/CISAN-FLACSO.

Estévez, Ariadna. 2017. "The biopolitics of asylum law in the United States." In *The Routledge Handbook of Biopolitics*, edited by Sergei Prozorov and Simona Rentea, 247–259. New York: Routledge.

Estévez, Ariadna. 2018a. "Biopolítica y necropolítica: ¿constitutivos u opuestos?" *Espiral, Estudios sobre Estado y Sociedad* 25 (73):9–43.

Estévez, Ariadna. 2018b. *Guerras necropolíticas y biopolítica de asilo en América del Norte*. Mexico: CISAN/UNAM-UACM.

Estévez, Ariadna. 2020. "Zoomism and Discipline for Productive Immobility," *Critical Legal Thinking. Law and the Political*, On line: https://criticallegalthinking.com/2020/05/13/zoomism-and-discipline-for-productive-immobility/. Accessed September 23, 2020.

Feline Freier, and Luisa Freier. 2013. Open doors (for almost all): visa policies and ethnic selectivity in Ecuador. Edited by Center for Comparative Immigration Studies.

Flores Pérez, Carlos Antonio. 2012. "La lógica del botín: de la cooptación del estado y el estado 'fallido.'" *Arenas. Revista Sinaloense de Ciencias Sociales* 13 (1):11–44.

Flores Pérez, Carlos Antonio. 2013. *Historias de polvo y sangre: génesis y evolución del tráfico de drogas en el estado de Tamaulipas*. México: CIESAS.

Forbes Staff. 2019. Violencia causa desplazamiento de 247,090 personas en Honduras de 2004 a 2018. FORBES. (December 11, 2019).

Foucault, Michel. 1977a. *Madness and Civilization. A History of Insanity in the Age of Reason*. Translated by Richard Howard. 3rd ed. London: Tavistock Publications. Original edition, 1961.

Foucault, Michel. 1977b. Va-t-on extrader Klaus Croissant? *Le Nouvel Observateur* (679):62–63. Accessed January 20, 2014.

Foucault, Michel. 1982. "Technologies of the self. Lectures at University of Vermont in October 1982." Foucault.info, accessed July 6, 2020. https://foucault.info/documents/foucault.technologiesOfSelf.en/.

Foucault, Michel. 1984. "De los espacios otros 'Des espaces autres,' Conferencia dicada en el Cercle des études architecturals, 14 de marzo de 1967." *Architecture, Mouvement, Continuité* (5).

Foucault, Michel. 1985. *The use of pleasure. The history of sexuality*. Translated by Robert Hurley. Three vols. Vol. II. Middlesex: Viking Penguin Books Ltd.

Foucault, Michel. 1988a. *The care of the self. The history of sexuality*. Translated by Robert Hurley. Edited by Paul Rabinow. Three vols. Vol. III, *The Foucault Reader*. London: Allen Lane, The Penguin Press. Original edition, 1984.

Foucault, Michel. 1988b. "El sujeto y el poder." *Revista Mexicana de Sociología* 50 (3):3–20.

Foucault, Michel. 1990. *The history of sexuality. An introduction*. Translated by Robert Hurley. Three vols. Vol. I. Middlesex: Vintage Books.

Foucault, Michel. 1997. *Ethics: subjectivity and truth*. Edited by Paul Rabinow. Vol. I, *The Essential Works of Michel Foucault: 1954-1984*. New York: The New Press, New York.

Foucault, Michel. 1998a. *Aesthetics, method, and epistemology*. Edited by Paul Rabinow. Vol. II, *Essential Works of Foucault (1954-1984)*. New York: The New Press.

Foucault, Michel. 1998b. *The will to knowledge. The history of sexuality*. Translated by Robert Hurley. Three vols. Vol. I, *History/Philosophy/Social Sciences*. London: Penguin. Original edition, 1976.

Foucault, Michel. 2000. *Power*. Edited by Paul Rabinow. Vol. III, *Essential Works of Foucault (1954-1984)*. New York: The New Press.

Foucault, Michel. 2002. *The archeology of knowledge (and the discourse on language)*. Translated by A. M. Sheridan Smith. *Routledge Classics*. London: Routledge. Original edition, 1969.

Foucault, Michel. 2004. *The birth of biopolitics*. New York: Picador-Palgrave Macmillan.

Foucault, Michel. 2006a. *Defender la sociedad*. México: Fonbdo de Cultura Económica.

Foucault, Michel. 2006b. *Seguridad, territorio, población*. México: Fondo de Cultura Económica.

Foucault, Michel. 2013. "Right of Death and Power Over Life." In *Biopolitics. A reader*, edited by Timothy Campbell and Adam Sitze, 41–60. London: Duke University Press.

Foucault, Michel, Michel Senellart, and Arnold I. Davidson. 2007. *Security, territory, population: Lectures at the College de France, 1977-78*. Basingstoke: Palgrave Macmillan.

Foucault, Michel, Michel Senellart, and Collège de France. 2008. *The birth of biopolitics: Lectures at the Collège de France, 1978-79*. Basingstoke England; New York: Palgrave Macmillan.

GAIPE. 2017. "Represa de violencia. El plan que asesinó a Berta Cáceres," in Gandini, Luciana, Fernando Lozano Ascencio, and Victoria Prieto. 2019. *Crisis y migración de población venezolana. Entre la desprotección y la seguridad jurídica en Latinoamérica*. Mexico: UNAM.

García, Sergio. 2011. "Asylum for Former Mexican Police Officers persecuted by the Narcos." *Boston College Third World Law Journal* 31 (2):245–267.

Gibney, Mark. 2000. "In Search of a US Refugee Policy." In *The United States and Human Rights. Looking Inward and Outward*, edited by David P. Forsythe, 52–72. Nebraska: University of Nebraska Press.

Giroux, Henry A. 2009. *Zombie politics and culture in the age of casino capitalismo*. Edited by Tobby Miller. NYC: Peter Lang.

Giroux, Henry. 2014. Neoliberalism and the Machinery of Disposability. *Truth-Out* (http://www.truth-out.org/opinion/item/22958-neoliberalism-and-the-machinery-of-disposability).

Global Witness. 2009. Illegal logging in the Río Plátano Biosphere. A farce in three acts.

Global Witness. 2015. ¿Cuántos más? El medio ambiente mortal de 2014: intimidación y asesinato de activistas ambientales y de la tierra, con Honduras en primer plano. Global Witness.

González Velázquez, Eduardo. 2011. *Frontera vertical: México frente a los migrantes centroamericanos*: UTEG.

Google Maps. 2020. "Mapa COVID 19 Coronavirus." Google Maps, accessed April 6, 2020. https://news.google.com/covid19/map?hl=es-419&gl=US&ceid=US:es-419.

Grillo, Ioan. 2014. Fracking near the Texas border has northern Mexico trembling. *The World* (http://www.pri.org/stories/2014-04-29/fracking-near-texas-border-has-northern-mexico-trembling). Accessed July 8, 2020.

Grosfoguel, Ramón. 2014. Racism, intersectionality and migration studies: framing some theoretical reflections. *Identities: Global Studies in Culture and Power*. L. Rivera Sánchez and F. Lozano Ascencio. London, Taylor and Francis.

Grosfoguel, Ramón. 2017. "Las migraciones coloniales del Caribe a Estados Unidos y Europa Occidental: colonialidades diferenciadas en cuatro centros del sistema-mundo." *Kamchatka. Revista de análisis cultural.* 9 (Julio 2017):225–250.

Gržinić, Marina, and Šefik Tatlić. 2014. *Necropolitics, racialization, and global capitalism. Historicization of biopolitics and forensics of politics, art, and life*. Lanham: Lexington Books.

Haraway, Donna. 1988. "Situated Knowledges: The Science Question in Feminism and the Privilege of Partial Perspective sheds light on Haraway's vision for a feminist science." *Feminist Studies* 14 (3):575–599. DOI:10.2307/317806.

Hardt, Michael, and Antonio Negri. 2000. *Empire*. Cambridge, Mass.; London: Harvard University Press.

Harman, Chris. 2009. *Zombie capitalism: global crisis and the relevance of Marx*. London: Bookmarks.

Harvey, David. 2004. "El nuevo imperialismo: acumulación por desposesión." *Socialist register* 2004:99–129.

Harvey, David. 2006. *Spaces of global capitalism*. London; New York, NY: Verso.

Hathaway, James C. 2005. *The rights of refugees under international law*. Cambridge: Cambridge University Press.

Healy, Sally, and Mark Bradbury. 2010. Endless war: a brief history of the Somali conflict. *Conciliation Resources*.

Henao Castro, Andrés Fabián. 2016. "From the 'Bio' to the 'Necro.' The Human at the Border." In *Resisting biopolitics: philosophical, political, and performative strategies,* edited by S. E. Wilmer and Audrone Zukauskaite, viii, 306 pages. New York: Routledge.

Hernández Cervantes, Aleida. 2015. *La producción jurídica de la globalización económica: notas de una pluralidad jurídica transnacional*. Mexico: CEIICH-UNAM.

Hernández Cervantes, Aleida. 2018. "Estructuras jurídicas del despojo: un caso de reforma estructural en México." In *Derecho, conflicto social y emancipación: Entre la depresión y la esperanza*, edited by Mauro Benente and Marco Navas Alvear, 41–56. Argentina: CLACSO.

Herrera Rosales, E. (2018). "El espacio, el tiempo y el racismo en las perspectivas decoloniales: apuntes para descolonizar los estudios sobre migración internacional." *Interdisciplina* 6(16):167–186.

Human Rights Watch. 2018. "Q&A: Trump Administration's 'Zero-Tolerance' Immigration Policy." Human Rights Watch, Last Modified, August 16, accessed July 10, 2020. https://www.hrw.org/news/2018/08/16/qa-trump-administrations-zero-tolerance-immigration-policy.

IDMC. 2016. 2016 Global Report on Internal Displacement. Internal Displacement Monitoring Centre.

IDMC. 2020a. HONDURAS. Displacement associated with Conflict and Violence Figure Analysis –GRID 2020. Geneva: Internal Displacement Monitoring Center.

IDMC. 2020b. MEXICO. Displacement associated with Conflict and Violence Figure Analysis –GRID 2020. Geneva: Internal Displacement Monitoring Center.

Insight Crime. 2018. "Honduras and Venezuela: Coup and Cocaine Air Bridge."

Jonas, Susan. 2013. Guatemalan Migration in Times of Civil War and Post-War Challenges. *Migration Policy Institute*.

Kaldor, Mary. 1999. *New and old wars: organized violence in a global era*. Stanford, Calif.: Stanford University Press.

Kaldor, Mary. 2006. *New & old wars*. 2nd ed. Cambridge: Polity.

Kao, Jason, and Denise Lu. 2019. How Trump's Policies Are Leaving Thousands of Asylum Seekers Waiting in Mexico. *The New York Times* (August 18, 2019): https://www.nytimes.com/interactive/2019/08/18/us/mexico-immigration-asylum.html. Accessed July 10, 2020.

Knox, Vickie. Forthcoming. "Violence, corruption and displacement in Honduras: From state indifference to state complicity."

Lagos Nivárrez, Agustín. 2015. Honduras tiene tres pulmones naturales. *El Heraldo* (June 13, 2005): https://www.elheraldo.hn/alfrente/849299-209/honduras-tiene-tres-pulmones-naturales.

Lakhani, Nina. 2020. *Who killed Berta Cáceres? Dams, death squads and an indigenous defender's battle for the planet*. London & New York: Verso.

Le Clercq Ortega, Juan Antonio, and Gerardo Rodríguez Sánchez Lara. 2016. Índice Global de impunidad México IGI-MEX 2016. Cholula, Puebla: Universidad de las Américas, Consejo Ciudadano de seguridad y Justicia de Puebla.

Lo Presti, Laura. 2019. "Terraqueous Necropolitics: Unfolding the low-operational, Forensic, and Evocative Mapping of Mediterranean Sea Crossings in the Age of Lethal Borders." *ACME: An International Journey for Critical Geographies* 18 (6):1347–1367.

López, Edgar. 2017. Oro y caos: una mafia está al mando del Arco Minero del Orinoco en Venezuela. *Insight Crime* (https://es.insightcrime.org/noticias/analisis/oro-caos-mafia-mando-arco-minero-orinoco-venezuela/).

Marchand, Marianne, and írez Ortega Ra, Adriana Sletza. 2019. "Globalising cities at the crossroads of migration: Puebla, Tijuana and Monterrey." *Third World Quarterly* 40 (3):612–632.

Martin, Susan. 2010. "Forced Migration, the Refugee Regime and the Responsibility to Protect." *Global Responsibility to Protect* 2 (2010):38–59.

Massey, Doreen. 2008. "A Global Sense of Place." In *The Cultural Geographer Reader*, edited by Timothy Oakes and Patricia L. Price, 260. NYC: Routledge.

Matta, Nelson, and Julio C. Herrera. 2019. Clan del Golfo tapona a migrantes en el Darién. *El Colombiano* (February 19, 2019).

Mayblin, L. 2017. *Asylum after empire: Colonial legacies in the politics of asylum seeking.* Lanham: Rowman & Littlefield.

Mayblin, L. 2020a. *Impoverishment and asylum: Social policy as slow violence.* London, Routledge.

Mayblin, L. 2020b. *Migration studies and colonialism.* Polity.

Mayblin, L., M. Wake, and M. Kazemi. 2020. "Necropolitics and the Slow Violence of the Everyday: Asylum Seeker Welfare in the Postcolonial Present." *Sociology* 54(1):107–123.

Mayorga, Patricia. 2014. "Narco 'ablandó' zona de Chihuahua rica en gas shale: Morena." In: Revista Proceso. https://www.proceso.com.mx/380107/narco-ablando-zona-de-chihuahua-rica-en-gas-shale-morena.

Mbembe, Achille. 2000. "At the Edge of the World: Boundaries, Territoriality, and Sovereignty in Africa." *Public Culture* 12 (1):259–284.

Mbembe, Achille. 2003. "Necropolitics." *Public Culture* 15 (1):11–40.

Mbembe, Achille. 2011. *Necropolítica*. España: Melusina (sic).

Mestries, Francis. 2014. Los desplazados internos forzados: refugiados invisibles en su propia patria. *El Cotidiano* (183):17–25.

Mezzadra, Sandro, and Brett Neilson. 2013. *Border as method, or the multiplication of labor*. Durham: Duke University Press.

Mix Migration Hub. 2018. "What is mix migration?" *MHub*. http://www.mixedmigrationhub.org/member-agencies/what-mixed-migration-is/.

Mohda, Saidatulakmal, Mohammad Darabi Golshani Irana, Abdelhak Senadjkib, Nur Azirah Zahida Mohamad Azhara, and Nurul Syifaa Mohd Shakila. 2016. "Pockets of Poverty: Who, Where, What and Why?" *Researchgate*. https://www.researchgate.net/publication/321183317_Pockets_of_Poverty_Who_Where_What_and_Why.

Monárrez Fragoso, Julia Estela. 2009. *Trama de una injusticia. Feminicidio sexual sistémico en Ciudad Juárez, Estudios de género*. Tijuana, BC: Colef-Porrúa.

Moscoso Rosero, Mafe. 2020. Guayaquil, "colonial virus." *El Salto Diario* (April 4, 2020): https://www.elsaltodiario.com/el-rumor-de-las-multitudes/guayaquil-colonial-virus.

Movimiento Migrante Mesoamericano. 2020. "Posicionamiento de las y los sobrevivientes al motín en la cárcel migratoria de Tenosique." Movimiento Migrante Mesoamericano. https://movimientomigrantemesoamericano.org/2020/04/03/posicionamiento-de-los-sobrevivientes-al-motin-en-la-carcel-migratoria-de-tenosique/?fbclid=IwAR0X7jubNsZG7kV5zN93lyd6izB0yumoj1GDWoiX15wqk5JCQgVIyTnuhs8.

MSF. 2019. "The struggle of Venezuelan migrants and asylum seekers in northern Brazil." Medicins Sans Frontiers, accessed August 27, 2020. https://www.msf.org/struggle-venezuelan-migrants-and-asylum-seekers-northern-brazil.

Musarò, Pierluigi. 2019. "European borderscapes: The management of migration between care and control." In *Global humanitarianism and media culture*, edited by Michael Lawrence and Rachel Tavernor, 145–166. Manchester University Press.

Narea, Nicole. 2019. The Trump administration will start sending migrants back to Guatemala under a new rule. *Vox* (November 19, 2019). Accessed July 10, 2020.

Negri, Antonio, Michael Hardt, Sandro Mezzadra, Mauro Cerbino, and Isabella Giunta. 2017. *Biocapitalismo, procesos de gobierno y movimientos sociales.*

Nixon, Rob. 2011. *Slow violence and the environmentalism of the poor.* Cambridge, Massachusetts: Harvard University Press.

O'Farrell, Clare. 2005. *Michel Foucault.* Sage.

Observatorio Venezolano de Violencia. 2019. Informe Anual de Violencia 2019.

Open Society. 2016. Atrocidades innegables. Confrontando crimenes de lesa humanidad en México. edited by Eric Witte. Nueva York: Open Society Foundation.

Ortega, José A. 2010. Cd. Juárez, por segundo año consecutivo, la ciudad más violenta del mundo. *Seguridad, justicia y paz* (11 de enero, 2010). Accessed 4 de septiembre, 2017.

Ortega Velázquez, Elisa. 2019. "Asilo: ¿derecho humano o prerrogativa del Estado?" *Revista Temas de Derechos Constitucional* 1 (1):55–82.

OSAC. 2019. Venezuela 2019 Crime & Safety Report. Edited by Department of State Bureau of Diplomatic Security. Washington, DC: Overseas Security Advisory Council.

Padgett, Humberto. 2014. *Las muertas del estado: feminicidios durante el gobierno mexiquense de Peña Nieto.* Grijalbo.

Paley, Dawn. 2014. *Drug war capitalism.* Oakland: AK Press.

Penn State Law. 2020. "Immigration in the Time of Trump." Penn State Law, accessed July 10, 2020. https://pennstatelaw.psu.edu/immigration-time-of-trump.

Pew Research Center. 2019. "For the fifth time in a row, the new Congress is the most racially and ethnically diverse ever," accessed July 10, 2020. https://www.pewresearch.org/fact-tank/2019/02/08/for-the-fifth-time-in-a-row-the-new-congress-is-the-most-racially-and-ethnically-diverse-ever/.

Pickering, Sharon. 2005. "Crimes of the State: the Persecution and Protection of Refugees." *Critical Criminology* 13:141–163.

Picozza, F. 2021. *The coloniality of asylum: Mobility, autonomy and solidarity in the Wake of Europe's Refugee Crisis.* Lanham: Rowman & Littlefield.

Pincheira T., Iván. 2012. "La gestión gubernamental de las emociones en el Chile neoliberal." *Revista Liminales. Escritos sobre Psicología y Sociedad. Universidad Central de Chile* 1 (1).

Polo Alvis, Sebastián, Enrique Serrano López, and Laura Manrique Lara. 2018. "Panorama de la frontera entre Colombia y Panamá: flujos migratorios e ilegalidad en el Darién." *Novum Jus* 13 (1):17–43.

Polzer, Tara. 2008. "Invisible Integration: How Bureaucratic, Academic and Social Categories Obscure Integrated Refugees." *Journal of Refugee Studies* 21: 476–497.

Pradilla, Alberto. 2019a. En frontera sur, 2,400 elementos de la Guardia; no detendrán a migrantes, asegura el gobierno. *Animal Politico* (June 17, 2020): https://www.animalpolitico.com/2019/06/guardia-nacional-migrantes-frontera-sur/.

Pradilla, Alberto. 2019b. ¿Qué pasó con los migrantes que llegaron a México hace un año en la caravana? *Animal Politico* (October 27, 2019): https://www.animalpolitico.com/2019/10/que-paso-migrantes-caravana-mexico/.

Price, Matthew. 2006. "Persecution Complex: Justifying Asylum Law's Preference for Persecuted People." *Harvard International Law Journal* 47 (2):413–446.

Proceso Digital. 2019. Más de 2 mil 500 hondureños están en condiciones de precariedad en Tijuana. *Proceso Digital* (January 5, 2019): https://www.proceso.hn/actualidad/7-actualidad/mas-de-2-mil-500-hondurenos-estan-en-condiciones-de-precariedad-en-tijuana.html.

Quijano, Aníbal. 2005. "Colonialidad del poder, eurocentrismo y América Latina." In *La colonialidad del saber: Perspectivas latinoamericanas*, edited by Edgardo Lander, 201–246. Buenos Aires: CLACSO.

Quijano, Aníbal. 2007. "Colonialidad del poder y clasificación social." In *El giro decolonial: reflexiones para una diversidad epistémica más allá del capitalismo global*, edited by Santiago Castro-Gómez and Ramón Grosfoguel, 285–327. Bogotá: Siglo del Hombre / Universidad Central / Insti-tuto de Estudios Sociales Contemporáneos y Pontificia Universidad Javeriana / Instituto Pensar.

Radford, Jill. 2006. "Introducción." In *Feminicidio. La política del asesinato de las mujeres*, edited by Diana E. Russell and Jill Radford, 33–52. México: CEIICH-UNAM/Cámara de Diputados.

Rajagopal, B. (1999). "Locating the Third World in Cultural Geograph." *Third World Legal Studies* 15 Postcolonialism, Globalization and Law(Article 2):1–20.

Ramji-Nogales, Jaya, Andrew I. Schoenholtz, and Philip G. Schrag. 2008. "Refugee Roulette: Disparities in Asylum Adjudication." *Stanford Law Review* 60 (2007):119.

Ramón, Paul. 2018. For Many Fleeing Venezuela's Chaos, New Trouble in Brazil. *National Geographic*: https://www.nationalgeographic.com/magazine/2018/11/dispatches-venezuela-migrants-brazil-warao-pacaraima/. Accessed August 27, 2020.

Recamier, Mariana. 2019. Migrantes africnos atrapados en México. *Reporte Índigo* (August 28, 2019): https://www.reporteindigo.com/latitud/migrantes-africanos-atrapados-en-mexico-protesta-transito-eu-represion-policia-federal/.

Redacción AN. 2016. Veracruz: 24 periodistas y fotógrafos asesinados en los últimos 11 años. *Aristegui Noticias* (August 4, 2016).

Redacción BBC Mundo. 2018. Caravana de migrantes en Tijuana: gases lacrimógenos y deportaciones, los enfrentamientos entre la patrulla fronteriza de EE.UU. y migrantes centroamericanos. *BBC Mundo* (November 26, 2018): https://www.bbc.com/mundo/noticias-america-latina-46339188.

Redacción El Heraldo de México. 2018. ¿Qué pasó con los migrantes haitianos en Tijuana? *El Heraldo de México* (Octover 27, 2018): https://heraldodemexico.com.mx/tendencias/que-paso-con-los-migrantes-haitianos-en-tijuana/.

Reed, Holly E., Bernadette Ludwig Ludwig, and Laura Braslow. 2016. "Forced Migration." In *International Handbook of Migration and Population Distribution*, edited by Michael J. White, 605–625. New York: Springer.

Refugees International. 2020. COVID-19 and the displaced: addressing the threat of the novel coronavirus in humanitarian emergencies. Refugees International.

Repo, Jemima. 2016. "Thanatopolitics or biopolitics? Diagnosing the racial and sexual politics of the European far-right." *Contemporary Political Theory* 15 (1):110–118.

Rivera, Rubén. 2020. México registró 34,582 asesinatos durante 2019, la cifra más alta en 20 años. *Univision Noticias* (January 21, 2020). Accessed July 6, 2020.

Robinson, Andy. 2020. *Oro, petróleo y aguacates: las nuevas venas abiertas de América Latina*. Primera edición. Barcelona: Arpa.

Rocío, Gallegos. 2018. 'Acampan' migrantes en puente de Ciudad Juárez, esperan asilo de EU. *La Verdad*: https://laverdadjuarez.com/index.php/2018/10/30/acampan-migrantes-en-puente-de-ciudad-juarez-esperan-asilo-de-eu/?fbclid=IwAR1pcxr8HkLN5u1O9xGk3pcjQY3epMK5NJ-7-hBB8c8PhZlFml0CWrmTVsw.

Rodríguez Cortés, Raúl. 2016. Los Moreira, Los Zetas y los campos de exterminio. *El Universal*.

Roitman Rosenmann, Marcos. 2005. *Las razones de la democracia en América Latina*. Mexico: Siglo XXI.

Romero Malgarejo, Osvaldo, and Alessa Pech Matamoros. 2014. "La violencia de los proxenetas en la prostitución de mujeres en la historia regional de los nahuas de la Malinche." In *Escenarios, realidades, e imaginarios en tiempos violentos*, edited by Ricardo Romano Garrido, Osvaldo Romero Melgarejo and Raúl Jiménez Guillén, 89–115. Tlaxcala: Universidad Autónoma de Tlaxcala.

Rose, Nicholas, Pat O' Malley, and Marian Valverde. 2006. "Governmentality." *Annual Review of Law and Social Science* (2):83–104.

Round, John, and Irina Kuznetsova. 2016. "Necropolitics and the Migrant as a Political Subject of Disgust: The Precarious Every Day of Russia's Labour Migrants." *Critical Sociology* 42 (3):1–18.

Roy, Arundhati. 2014. *Capitalism: a ghost story*. Chicago, IL: Haymarket Books.

Ruiz, Francisco Javier. 2018. El Arco Minero del Orinoco Diversificación del extractivismo y nuevos regímenes biopolíticos. *Nueva Sociedad*.

Segato, Rita Laura. 2006. *Ciudad Juárez. Territorio, soberanía y crímenes de segundo estado*. Argentina: Tinta Limón.

Segato, Rita Laura. 2014. "Las nuevas formas de la guerra y el cuerpo de las mujeres." *Sociedade e Estado* 29 (2):341–371.

Shacknove, Andrew E. 1985. "Who Is a Refugee?" *Ethics* 95 (2):274–284.

Soja, Edward E. 2009. "The City and Spatial Justice." *Justice Spatiale/ Spatial Justice* 1 (1):5.

Sokhi-Bulley, Bal. 2011. "Government(ality) by Experts: Human Rights as Governance." *Law & Critique*, 22 (3):251–271.

Souza, Dalia. 2020. 61 mil 637 personas permanecen desaparecidas en México. *Somoes el medio* (January 18, 2020).

Squire, V. 2009. *The exclusionary politics of asylum*. Basingstoke, England; New York: Palgrave Macmillan.

Squire, Vicki. 2017. "Governing migration through death in Europe and the US: Identification, burial and the crisis of modern humanism." *European Journal of International Relations* 23 (3):513–532.

Stoker, Gerry. 1998. "Governance as theory: five propositions." *International Social Science Journal* (50):17–28.

Stümer, Jenny. 2018. "The Dead are Coming: Border Politics and Necropower in Europe." *Cultural Politics 14*(1): 20–39. https://doi.org/10.1215/17432197-4312856

Suárez, Karina. 2019. Mexico pone en marcha un programa para buscar a 40.000 desaparecidos. *El País* (Febrero 4, 2019): https://elpais.com/internacional/2019/02/04/mexico/1549301318_972191.html. Accessed May 1, 2019.

Swales, Vanessa. 2020. Immigrants Could Face Nearly $1,000 Charge to Appeal Deportation Orders. *The New York Times* (February 27, 2020): https://www.nytimes.com/2020/02/27/us/immigration-court-deportation-appeals.html. Accessed July 10, 2020.

Tazzioli, M. 2020. *The Making of Migration*. London, Sage.

Teran Mantovani, Emiliano. 2019. Venezuela and the Geo-Ecopolitics of Gold. *Venezuelanalysis.com* (August 19, 2020): https://venezuelanalysis.com/analysis/14630.

Terminski, Bogumil. 2018. Trump rejects 'global governance' in UN speech as he attacks Iran for 'sowing chaos.' *The Independent*. Accessed November 13.

The New York Times. 2017. Full Executive Order Text: Trump's Action Limiting Refugees Into the U.S. *The New York Times* (January 27, 2017): https://www.nytimes.com/2017/01/27/us/politics/refugee-muslim-executive-order-trump.html.

The United States Department of Justice. 2018. Attorney General Announces Zero-Tolerance Policy for Criminal Illegal Entry. Edited by Office of Public Affairs. Washington, DC: Department of Justice.

The White House. 2017a. Executive Order: Border Security and Immigration Enforcement Improvements. Edited by The President's Office. Washington, DC: The White House.

The White House. 2017b. Executive Order: Enhancing Public Safety in the Interior of the United States. Edited by The President's Office. Washington, DC: The White House.

The White House. 2018. Executive Order: Affording Congress an Opportunity to Address Family Separation. Edited by The President's Office. Washington, DC: The White House.

Tokar, Brian, and Gary Oliver. 1998. "The Texas-Vermont-Maine Nuclear Dump: Bringing Environmental Racism Home." Institute for Social Ecology. https://social-ecology.org/wp/1998/10/the-texas-vermont-maine-nuclear-dump-bringing-environmental-racism-home/.

Treviño Rangel, Javier. 2020. "Mercancías desechables: políticas de muerte y migración internacional en México." In *Necropolítica y migración en la frontera vertical mexicana. Un ejercicio de conocimiento situado*, edited by Ariadna Estévez and Elisa Ortega.

Tyner, James. 2019. *Dead Labor. Toward a political economy of premature death.* Minneapolis: Minnesota University Press.

U.S. Department of Homeland Security. 2017. "Office of Immigration Statistics." 44.

UN Commission on Human Rights. 1998. Guiding Principles on Internal Displacement. In *E/CN.4/1998/53/Add.2*, edited by ECOSOC. New York: United Nations.

UNCHR. 2015. Women on the run. First hand accounts of refugees fleeing El Salvador, Guatemala, Honduras, and Mexico. 60. Accessed August 27, 2016.

UNHCR. 2013. UNHCR Statistical Online Population Database: Sources, Methods and Data Considerations. Edited by UNHCR.

UNHCR. 2018. UNCHR Statistics - The World in Numbers. Edited by UNCHR. Geneva.

UNCHR. 2020. Global Trends. Forced Displacement in 2020. In *Publications*, edited by UNCHR. Geneva: United Nations.

United Nations. 2020. "Quarantine halts migrants in Panama." https://www.un.org/en/coronavirus/quarantine-halts-migrants-panam%C3%A1?fbclid=IwAR1bBgmSMJGj_9TZGEUAZcE_IbNfXUnaczCNCyBFTHCc0DvSnj5_Tbpx1uI.

United Nations Office on Drugs and Crime. 2010. The Globalization of Crime: a Transnational Organized Crime Threat Assessment Viena: United Nations Office on Drugs and Crime.

United Nations Office on Drugs and Crime. 2012. Transnational Organized Crime in Central America and the Caribbean: A Threat Assessment. Vienna: United Nations Office on Drugs and Crime.

United Nations Office on Drugs and Crime. 2019. Global Study on Homicide. Executive Summary. Vienna: United Nations Office on Drugs and Crime.

Valencia, Sayak. 2010. *Capitalismo Gore*. España: Melusina.

Valero Martínez, Mario. 2018. "Venezuela, migraciones y territorios fronterizos." *Línea Imaginaria. Revista de Investigación de Estudios Sociales y de Frontera* 6 (3):http://portal.amelica.org/ameli/jatsRepo/62/62586002/html/index.html.

Valverde Gefaell, Clara. 2016. *De la necropolítica Neoliberal, A la Empatía Radical. Violencia Discreta, Cuerpos Excluidos y Repolitización*. Madrid: Icaria.

Varela Huerta, Amarela. 2017. "Las masacres de migrantes en San Fernando y Cadereyta: dos ejemplos de gubernamentalidad necropolítica." *Iconos. Revista de Ciencias Sociale. FLACSO Andes* (58):131–149.

Varela Huerta, Amarela. 2020. *Necropolítica y migración en la frontera vertical mexicana. Un ejercicio de conocimiento situado*. Edited by Ariadna Estévez and Elisa Ortega Velázquez. Mexico: Instituto de Investigaciones Jurídicas UNAM.

Vaughan-Williams, Nick. 2015. *Europe's Border crisis: Biopolitical security and beyond*. Oxford: Oxford Scholarship Online.

Verité. 2016. The Nexus of Illegal Gold Mining Supply Chains. Amherst: Verité. Fair Labor Worldwide.

Vice News. 2015. Ayotzinapa: A Timeline of the Mass Disappearance That Has Shaken Mexico. *www.vice.com* (https://www.vice.com/en_us/article/bja4xa/ayotzinapa-a-timeline-of-the-mass-disappearance-that-has-shaken-mexico). Accessed July 6, 2020.

Wainwright, Tom. 2016. *Narconomics: how to run a drug cartel*. First edition. New York: PublicAffairs.

Walia, H. (2021). *Border & rule: Global migration, capitalism, and the rise of racist nationalism*. Chicago, Illinois: Haymarket Books.

Wallace, Beth, 2018. "Necropolitics in Refugee Governance." *Granite Journal: a Postgraduate. Interdisciplinary Journal:* (2):9–17.

Waslin, Michele. 2020. "The Use of Executive Orders and Proclamations to Create Immigration Policy: Trump in Historical Perspective." *Journal on Migration and Human Security* 8 (1):54–67.

Wintour, Patrick. 2017. Donald Trump pulls US out of UN global compact on migration. *The Guardian*. Accessed November 12, 2018.

Woodiwiss, Michael. 2005. *Gangster capitalism: the United States and the global rise of organized crime*. London: Constable.

Yeoman, Barry. 2015. The Uncounted. On India's Coast, A Power Plant Backed By The World Bank Group Threatens A Way Of Life. *Huffington Post* (May 1, 2015). Accessed November 16, 2018.

Zetter, Roger. 2007. "More labels, fewer refugees: Remaking the Refugee Label in an Era of Globalization." *Journal of Refugee Studies* 20 (2):172–192.

Zolberg, Aristide. 1983. "The Formation of New States as a Refugee-Generating Process." *The ANNALS of the American Academy of Political and Social Science* 467:89–101.

Zylinska, Joanna. 2004. "The Universal Acts: Judith Butler and the biopolitics of immigration." *Cultural Studies* 18 (4):523–537.

Index

About the Author

Ariadna Estévez is a tenured research professor at the Centre for Research on North America (CISAN) of the National Autonomous University of Mexico (UNAM). She holds a Ph.D. in International Relations (mention in Human Rights) (University of Sussex, UK). She teaches the courses The Necropolitical Apparatus of Forced Migration and Research Seminar on Biopolitics and Necropolitics at UNAM's Faculty of Political and Social Sciences. She is co-coordinator of the Research in Progress Seminar on Critical Legal Studies and Migration at UNAM's Institute of Legal Research (CISAN-IIJ). She is the author of *Necropolitical Wars and the Biopolitics of Asylum in North America* (2018) and *Human Rights, Migration and Social Conflict: Towards a Decolonized Global Justice* (2012). She is also the editor of *Necropower in North America, The Legal Spatialization of Disposability and Lucrative Death* (2021), and *9 Reasons to (Dis)Trust Human Rights* (2017).

www.ingramcontent.com/pod-product-compliance
Lightning Source LLC
LaVergne TN
LVHW091533200926
848483LV00002B/389